"*Agile Leadership for Turbulent Times* cuts to the chase. It challenges traditional leadership thinking and offers an intriguing alternative approach to redefine our 'new normal' post-COVID-19 world!"

—*Marshall Goldsmith,* New York Times *#1 bestselling author of* Triggers, Mojo, *and* What Got You Here Won't Get You There

"This is such a timely book. Among so many books on leadership, this one stands on its own level, almost as though it has been written from the future. Sharon, Frederick and Colin have re-envisioned leadership in an entirely new way, creating a deeply accessible and inspiring roadmap for a new kind of leader. In the challenging times that lie ahead, we cannot move forwards by thinking in the same way as we used to. Now we need something entirely new, something that has never been done before, and for that, we need a new leader. This book is for those who dare to throw away the old deck of cards and step into a whole new world."

—*Richard Rudd, author and founder of Gene Keys*

"Ego, eco and intuitive intelligence: a great way to frame a leader's challenges and responses."

—*Gert de Winter, Group CEO, Bâloise*

"Olivier, Hölscher and Williams have captured the essence of what works when leading in today's unpredictable world."

—*Jan-Erik Kjerpeseth, CEO, Sparebanken Vest*

"This extraordinary leadership book is an essential read. The authors pool their vast experience from boardroom, classroom, field research and client experience, in an easy-to-digest yet groundbreaking approach that deals with the root causes of today's 21st century leadership challenges."

—*Giles Hutchins, Chair of The Future Fit Leadership Academy, author of* Future Fit *and* Regenerative Leadership

"*Agile Leadership for Turbulent Times* distils the essence of good leadership in a complex environment in a very innovative and fresh way. I found this book indeed to be very helpful and relevant to my job as a company leader."

—*Cristiano Venturini, CEO, iGuzzini illuminazione S.p.A*

"*Agile Leadership for Turbulent Times* is perhaps the most apt leadership book for the new disrupted world we find ourselves in. Identifying an accessible framework of leadership intelligence with practical application."

—*Sophie Dekkers, Scheduling Director, EasyJet*

"Change is situational, transformation is psychological. This important book provides a compelling framework to support leaders in their transitions by decoding complexity in a helpful, practical and engaging fashion. Truly: not to be missed."

—*Paolo Gallo, author of* The Compass & The Radar

"Leadership – not easy but not complicated. *Agile Leadership for Turbulent Times* distils the essence of good leadership in a complex environment. I fully recommend this book for practising leaders."

—*Simon Western, Chief Executive Analytical-Network Coaching, Adjunct Professor, University College Dublin, author of* Leadership: A Critical Text

"This book made me pause and review my assumptions and beliefs about leadership: what works and what doesn't. It provides practical tips for leading in uncertainty."

—*Kai Siedlatzek, Head of Product Controlling, AUDI AG*

"This book invites us to stop and think through our assumptions about leadership. It provides interesting insights for a more effective approach for uncertain times."

—*Pierre Lourens, CEO of the Impala Bafokeng Trust – Impala Platinum*

"This book on Eco, Ego, and Intuitive intelligences captures the essence of what works when leading in today's unpredictable world: it could not be more relevant."

—*Heather McElwee, Executive Director, Pittsburg Glass Center*

"This book provides a refreshing new way to frame ideas and research around leadership – drawing on their own experience, and that of colleagues and business school participants, Olivier,

Hölscher and Williams weave stories and academic research into a compelling dialogue."
—*Vicki Culpin, Professor of Organisational Behaviour, Hult International Business School*

"*Agile Leadership for Turbulent Times* challenges traditional thinking about leadership and offers an intriguing alternative approach."
—*Robert Kovach, PhD, Director, Critical Leaders & Teams, People & Communities, Cisco*

"The authors manage to reduce the complexity of leadership by using an uncommon amount of common sense."
—*Peter Burman, President, Corporate Solutions at EF Education First*

"Finally, an exciting, new 2021 perspective on intelligence: essential for leaders and individuals in the new world of work. The authors are to be commended."
—*Peter Lawrence, former CEO and Board Advisor*

"This book strongly stimulates leaders to give their best and grow beyond the ordinary! A fantastic framework reflecting on all facets of leadership, and finally including the always missing piece of the puzzle – intuitive intelligence. A must-read for agile leadership!"
—*Annabelle Mieth, Advanced Business Development and Marketing, Continental Corporation*

"The Old World is no more. A New World awaits us. This book will help leaders navigate uncharted waters."
—*Satish Roopa, Council Member, Da Vinci Institute: School of Business Leadership. Committee Member, Independent Commission for the Remuneration of Public Office Bearers.*

"Olivier, Hölscher and Williams invite us to stop, to think and to review our assumptions about agile leadership in a world which demands more agility than ever. Drawing on a broad theoretical underpinning this book is for leaders at all levels who are relishing the daily challenge being their best for others. It provides a great framework and interesting insights on how to master 3 leadership intelligences – ego, eco, intuitive – for a more effective approach for uncertain times!"
—*John Firth, Founder and CEO, The Firth Group*

AGILE LEADERSHIP FOR TURBULENT TIMES

This thought-provoking and engaging book is for you, whatever your seniority, in the private or public sector – if you are curious about the role and purpose of leadership in a turbulent world.

It will help you become a more agile leader through understanding and integrating your ego, eco and intuitive intelligence. You will gain a deeper understanding of your unique leadership blend through a short diagnostic inventory, bringing insight about your strengths and what may be tripping you up. The book offers tips, ideas and practical suggestions on how to develop your ability to use the three intelligences in order to expand your leadership repertoire. It will help you enable the teams you lead to be more flexible, responsive and autonomous.

The authors have drawn on their vast experience from the boardroom to the shop floor, the classroom and research around the world, to write an easy-to-digest yet ground-breaking book that deals with the root causes of today's twenty-first-century leadership challenges. Its contents are straightforward and widely applicable.

Sharon Olivier is Senior Faculty and Consultant in Leadership and HR Development at Hult Ashridge Executive Education. She is a contributing author of *Inspiring Leadership* and *Diamonds in the Dust*.

Frederick Hölscher, PhD, is a visiting professor at various business schools, and Adjunct Faculty at Hult Ashridge Executive Education. He is editor of *Diamonds in the Dust* and contributing author of *Inspiring Leadership* and *Development is for People*.

Colin Williams is Professor of Practice and Adjunct Faculty at Hult Ashridge Executive Education. He is founder and Director of Williams Leadership Development Ltd and co-author of *Living Leadership: A Practical Guide for Ordinary Heroes*.

AGILE LEADERSHIP FOR TURBULENT TIMES

Integrating Your Ego, Eco and Intuitive Intelligence

SHARON OLIVIER, FREDERICK HÖLSCHER AND COLIN WILLIAMS

Routledge
Taylor & Francis Group

LONDON AND NEW YORK

First published 2021
by Routledge
2 Park Square, Milton Park, Abingdon, Oxon OX14 4RN

and by Routledge
52 Vanderbilt Avenue, New York, NY 10017

Routledge is an imprint of the Taylor & Francis Group, an informa business

British Library Cataloguing-in-Publication Data
A catalogue record for this book is available from the British Library

Library of Congress Cataloging-in-Publication Data
Names: Olivier, Sharon, author. | Hölscher, Frederick, 1948– author. | Williams, Colin, 1954– author.
Title: Agile leadership for turbulent times: integrating your ego, eco and intuitive intelligence / Sharon Olivier, Frederick Hölscher and Colin Williams.
Description: Abingdon, Oxon; New York, NY: Routledge, 2021. | Includes bibliographical references and index.
Subjects: LCSH: Leadership—Psychological aspects. | Ego (Psychology)
Classification: LCC HD57.7 .O4325 2021 (print) | LCC HD57.7 (ebook) | DDC 658.4/092—dc23
LC record available at https://lccn.loc.gov/2020033195
LC ebook record available at https://lccn.loc.gov/2020033196

ISBN: 978-0-367-45710-5 (hbk)
ISBN: 978-0-367-62096-7 (pbk)
ISBN: 978-1-003-02959-5 (ebk)

Typeset in Helvetica Neue
by codeMantra

Agile leadership: The dance of the ego, eco and intuition

A call from the darkness….. entropy, formlessness, density, chaos.
Let there be light!
And so, the ego calls a world into being,
With its thoughts, with its voice, with its hands,
it shapes the formlessness…..
No-thingness into somethingness

From the denseness of her creative womb,
The eco releases them as they are called, idea after idea
But holds them with outstretched arms,
Keen not to lose the unity within the diversity
Reminding them to integrate as they are part of something bigger

Intuition tunes into the music and lets the rhythm flow
It takes the notes and strings them into
beautiful melodies never heard before
It cherishes the pauses between the notes
It is in those precious moments of silence
that the symphony of life is born

Enjoy the music and learn to dance to its rhythm!
Frederick Hölscher

CONTENTS

ACKNOWLEDGEMENTS

We would like to recognise the contribution of several people to the creation of this book. In different ways they have been discussion partners, champions and supporters. They have given us helpful feedback on early drafts and challenged us to deliver!

As this book draws on extensive experience as well as a recent research project, the list could be long. However, we are restricting ourselves to thanking those who have helped us during the time of the research and writing the book.

All the research participants, who willingly shared their stories, particularly Gert de Winter, Achim Wolter and the leadership team from Bâloise, Andrew Jones and leaders from TVS Supply Chain Solutions, and the leadership team of Oxford Analytica.

Kerrie Fleming and Vicki Holton, our co-researchers and co-authors of the research report Ego, Eco and Intuitive Leadership…a New Logic for Disruptive Times.

Our colleagues at Hult Ashridge Executive Education, particularly, Amy Bradley, Vicki Culpin, Dina Dommett, Sam Wilkinson, Carina Schofield, Nadine Page and Lee Waller for their contributions, feedback and encouragement.

Paul Griffith, for championing the radical redesign of the Transformational Leader programme which refined and 'road-tested' some of the ideas presented in this book.

All the participants who have attended the Transformational Leader programme at Ashridge. You played such an important role in helping to test and ground our thinking in real life leadership practices and challenges.

Giles Hutchins, who has worked with us, challenged us, encouraged and helped us develop our thinking. We are indebted to him and appreciate his generosity, and the sharing of his beautiful space in nature where we reflected and shared together.

John Higgins, for his enthusiastic encouragement to get on and write this book.

Peter Lawrence, former CEO of the first global consulting firm that Sharon and Frederick worked for, who had foresight and opened the door for them to develop some of what is offered in this book, in many organisations globally.

John Firth, a previous student, business owner and CEO of numerous companies who has applied what he has learned in the classroom with great success and who has kindly shared some of his stories.

Richard Rudd, not only for his eloquent and inspirational writing but for the many personal discussions and support. He is a great example of someone who has tuned into new realities and connected the dots in fresh new ways!

Claudius van Wyk, who introduced us to Holism and Spiral Dynamics. We had so many insightful discussions where he stretched our thinking and took us on conceptual journeys, as only he can do.

Danah Zohar, international author and thought leader in Quantum Leadership, for the contribution she has made to our thinking.

Colleagues and friends from South Africa who have inspired, challenged and supported us along the journey to producing this book; Deon van Zyl, Maryanne Smith, Satish Roopa, Kaizer Thibedi and Pierre Lourens.

Matthew Seaman at Friction3 for his help, insight and patience with design and illustrations.

Scabage.com for the cartoons. We loved how he was able to bring humour and expression to the concepts.

To each other as co-writers of this book. We have deepened our friendships and discovered an interesting blend of ego, eco and intuitive intelligence between the three of us...it has been quite an adventure!

There are too many others to mention – but thank you all!

Introduction

This short introduction explains the background to the book: the authors' motivation for writing it and an explanation of the research project underpinning it. It includes a guide on how to read this book and a brief explanation of the contents of each chapter.

About this book

This book is for you – the leader, or rather the person, with leadership responsibilities. You who are both relishing and terrified by the challenges in your working life today. It is written with the practising manager in mind.

We, Sharon, Frederick and Colin, have worked for many years as leaders. We have worked in different industries and in a variety of countries. We are now based in an international business school, but we continue to interact day in, day out, with leaders in organisations around the world. What we offer you in this book is a combination of our life-long learning journeys and more recent academic research into leadership. We invite you to test our ideas against your own, and then integrate and expand them in a way that makes sense to you.

This book is not a set of steps to deal with disruption or an easy recipe to become more agile. It offers a new narrative or framework for thinking about the nature of work and leadership, in the light of the current disruptive times.

During our immersive leadership development workshops, participants have found the vocabulary appealing, and easy to grasp and use. They have reported that it helps them take a closer look at their own leadership approach and helps explain why this has not always worked for them. It has enabled them to experiment with new approaches.

This framework seems to resonate with what they already know intuitively but never had a language for. One leader on a programme recently said, "I have been leading in this way (intuitively) for years and feeling unsure of myself, I am so relieved that it is a recognised approach!" Leaders have said that this framework helps them clarify their personal leadership approach and identify their development needs – and those of their organisation. More importantly, it enables them to see how their own 'stuckness' in a particular leadership approach may be causing a lack of agility in how they lead. Some leaders have adopted the three capability areas of ego, eco and intuitive as their organisational leadership development framework.

Although our work is deeply rooted in theory, the theory is not needed to grasp the essence of the framework. For those readers who like the theoretical underpinnings, we have offered a 'deeper dive' section at the end of some of the chapters. But for us the focus is more on practical application and usefulness to leaders in organisations. The biggest indicator of the value of our work lies in how it resonates with you the reader, and how it plays a part in contributing to your personal learning journey.

The research

The research project involved more than 250 senior leaders across a range of industries and of different nationalities over a four-year period. It included in-depth one-to-one interviews, group discussions, surveys, observation in the workplace and data collection in the classroom from participants on leadership pro- grammes. The conclusions were published by Hult Ashridge Executive Education in 2019 in the report 'Ego, Eco and Intuitive Leadership…a new logic for disruptive times'[1].

The research findings showed that new approaches to leadership are being experimented with in many organisations as old leader- ship recipes prove less effective. We explored and tested a new leadership logic with research participants. The thinking behind this logic originated from a combination of our practical experi- ence with an in-depth study of the literature on various leadership intelligences.

We created a new leadership typology based on three sense or meaning-making modes which in turn influence mindset and capabilities. We show how these can be explored as ego, eco and intuitive intelligence in the world of work. This framework moves beyond the traditional paradigms of scientific management, the behavioural sciences and emotional intelligence (EQ) to draw on the logic and wisdom of complexity thinking. If you would like to read the complete report it is available at https://www.hult.edu/en/ executive-education/insights/ego-eco-and-intuitive-leadership/

In this book we will:

- Help you understand ego, eco and intuitive leadership intel- ligence
- Enable you to identify your own preferences or approach, includ- ing its gifts (strengths) and shadows (weaknesses) through a short diagnostic inventory
- Take you on a deeper exploration of your own development journey to discover your unique strengths and what might be tripping you up
- Offer you tips, ideas and practical suggestions on how to develop your ability to use all three intelligences in order to expand your leadership repertoire and increase your leadership agility
- Help you preserve or evolve your organisation's culture and deal with the potential misalignment between leadership style and organisational culture

How to read this book: a reader's guide

Feel free to start at the beginning and finish at the end! However, if you are short of time, or want some guidance about where to focus first, then hopefully this short explanation of the chapters will help you get to the parts you will find most interesting.

Chapter 1 (The quest for agility in turbulent times) reviews the quest for agility in the face of the disruptive challenges facing leaders in the twenty-first century. It examines some of the common ways in which leaders have chosen to respond. It explains the limitations of some of the responses and offers some thoughts as to why we need to 'reframe' our perspective on leadership.

Chapter 2 (Rethinking leadership) explains our thinking in more depth. It introduces the theoretical underpinning and outlines the key concepts and frameworks used in the book. *Skip from chapter 1 to chapter 3 if you are more interested in 'how to' than 'why'!*

Chapter 3 (Ego intelligence: the shaper) challenges the popular contemporary notion that ego leadership is a bad thing. Clearly it can be unhelpful if overused, but a leader must be able to demonstrate the positive benefits of ego intelligence – clear thinking, focus, drive, energy and a willingness to make things happen. We call this the constructive use of the benevolent ego.

Chapter 4 (Intuitive intelligence: the sensor) focuses on unleashing our intuitive intelligence. It explores what we mean by intuition and 'sensing into and sensing beyond'. It reinforces the need for divergent thinking spaces and creativity at an individual and collective level. It also looks at what those who believe they are 'not intuitive' (a bit like people who feel they are 'not creative') can do to develop or enhance their ability to work in this way.

Chapter 5 (Eco intelligence: the integrator) explores the importance of eco intelligence as an essential integrating force. Although the concept of an organisation as a living ecosystem is broadly accepted the implications for leadership are less widely understood. The leader's role is to release the organisation's energy and to engage the collective intelligence of those around them. To do this some new skills and competences are necessary: we look at what these are.

Chapter 6 (The personal development journey) takes a deep dive into the reader's personal development journey. Its focus is on the ego development journey, ego-stuckness, the process of 'individuation' and how to develop a good blend of benevolent ego, eco and intuitive intelligence.

Chapter 7 (Leadership and cultural agility) looks at reciprocal relationship between leadership and organisational culture as two sides of a coin and explores how leaders can work with all three intelligences to either preserve or evolve culture in their organisations.

Chapter 8 (Being an agile leader) concentrates on how to be an agile leader by either integrating the three intelligences personally or through tapping into the distributed leadership in the organisation to create the right blend within the team. It offers you, as reader, a self-assessment diagnostic to understand your personal blend of the three intelligences.

The 'Deeper Dive' sections at the end of Chapters 3, 4, 5 and 7 provide additional information about the people and the concepts that have inspired and informed our thinking. They are not essential reading to follow the flow of the book.

Note

1 Olivier, S., Fleming, K., Hölscher, F., and Holton, V. (2019) Ego, eco and intuitive leadership...a new logic for disruptive times. *Hult International Business School*.

Chapter 1

The quest for agility in a turbulent world

Disruption is the teacher, not the enemy, of agile leaders

A disrupted world

When Frederick was a child, his father told him a story about a river frothing and foaming in full flood during a storm. He described how a huge tree cracked, then snapped under the weight of the water. But the reeds near the riverbank bent and bowed in the torrent, their roots holding them anchored in place. The next day the reeds recovered and stretched themselves up towards the sky, while the remains of the tree were carried away downstream. Perhaps you know this story from Aesop's fables?

Some leaders try to stand firm against the flood. They believe in 'tightening the nuts and bolts,' reinforcing their control until the storm passes. Other leaders are prepared to bend, to flex and to be agile in turbulent times. They seek new connections and contacts and have their antennae out, exploring weak signals of changes in their environment that may provide new opportunities.

The world today is every bit as turbulent as the storm described by Aesop. Leaders and their organisations, must have the ability to respond creatively to unpredictable challenges and opportunities. The need for agility has never been greater.

Looking at the macro picture today, we see three spheres of disruption which are all interdependent: technological, social and natural. All three present both threats and opportunities, and highlight the need for agility in individual and organisational responses.

Technological disruption

Social media, the internet of things (IoT), big data, artificial intelligence (AI), machine learning and many more technological disruptors are present in our daily lives. Shoshana Zuboff (2019)[1] talks about the emergence of 'surveillance capitalism': how personal data has become commoditised by mass surveillance of the internet to the extent that it, together with other elements, like AI, almost replaces human labour as the key asset of businesses. For many organisations and societies, data has become of primary importance. To paraphrase Vladimir Putin[2] (2017), "The nation that controls artificial intelligence will control the world." Business 'as usual' is gone forever.

The availability of data and advances in AI have accelerated decision-making: sometimes taking it out of the hands of leaders.

These various technological disruptions have a continuing impact on our social and cultural lives. Values are shifting as we learn to reconnect with each other in new ways. Klaus Schwab (2017)[3] of the World Economic Forum said, "the Fourth Industrial Revolution brought us to a place where we have to reconsider what it means to be human." We add to this imperative the need to rethink the place and role of leadership, and leader's ability to deal with paradoxes in a more agile way.

On the one hand, technology challenges how we work and live together, but on the other hand it is helping: how would we have coped during the coronavirus pandemic without the internet, social media and the IoT?

Social disruption

As well as being affected by technological disruption, social disruption has its own dynamics. A fundamental human paradox that impacts the way we work and our leadership is our human need for *belonging* and our need for *freedom*. As human beings we are social animals. We like to feel involved and be part of things and yet we have a strong need for self-expression and self-determination.

While the twentieth century will go down in history as the culmination of the age of liberation and individual expression, the twenty-first century is witnessing the return of a need for belonging and connectedness.

Hence the success of social media and the rise of what has been called Generation C – the connected generation. Information travels far and fast, boosting the development of our collective consciousness.

Another paradox is the tension between human desire for *stability and continuity* on the one hand, and our need for *change and innovation* on the other. We have a need to conserve our world, clinging to our traditions and values of the past, and on the other hand we are curious about a new future.

Natural disruption

The consumerist culture that drives the major economies of the world has had an almost irreversible impact on nature. For years we have been observing the consequences of global warming and the over-exploitation of our natural resources. According to IPCC (2014)[4] scientists and climate change experts say that this will lead to:

- Extremely high temperatures
- Sea levels rising 1–4 feet by 2100
- Ocean acidification affecting marine organisms
- Heavier rainfall, hurricanes, storm and floods
- Melting of snow and ice caps which could release catastrophic levels of methane gases creating run away climate change

Within these crises, another paradox has become a massive focus area in the world today – how to achieve economic prosperity, whilst protecting the planet? The United Nations has rightfully urged countries and businesses of the world to follow the Sustainable Development Goals (SDGs) and to promote prosperity while protecting the planet. They recognise that ending poverty must go hand-in-hand with strategies that build economic growth and address a range of social needs including education, health, social protection and job opportunities, whilst tackling climate change and environmental protection.

However, it is not only the macro challenges that call for action, but micro phenomena like the invisible COVID-19 virus are also having a significant impact on our macro-economics. As we write, we are in lockdown isolation which makes us deeply aware of the natural disruptions that face us in the twenty-first century.

Perhaps Mother Earth is reacting to the thoughtlessness and lack of consideration of human beings?

COVID-19 has put into vivid focus the vulnerability and the capacity for innovation in our socio-cultural ecosystems. Fear of contamination has put people worldwide into isolation, and surprisingly innovative ways of connecting and working together have emerged. For example, companies that resisted staff working from home for years have changed their policies over a weekend. Now they are discovering that people are more productive working without the constant interruptions of office life. On top of that they are saving travel and accommodation costs and giving Mother Nature a chance to get her breath back! Many organisations are now sensing a need to relook at their leadership approach and competency frameworks as their assumptions about home working, empowerment, trust and collaboration are being fundamentally challenged.

> The Managing Director of a technology company we work with explained that he had always insisted on his people working on site in order to monitor their productivity. He was astonished to report that since his team has worked from home, they have had their highest billing month in the history of the company!

Letting go of traditional recipes

In the face of the current uncertainties, most leaders will feel a level of fear – not to do so would be irresponsible. Yet in periods of uncertainty, leaders need curiosity and the confidence to seek new opportunities, explore different solutions and look for positive steps rather than resorting to allocating blame or being frozen into inaction. We describe this curiosity as 'seeking for diamonds in the dust' of disruption. This book is written for leaders who are curious: curiosity enables one to find these diamonds and to learn – and learning is essential to leadership.

To paraphrase Einstein,[5] "We can't solve problems by using the same kind of thinking we used when we created them."

Ego, eco and intuitive leadership intelligence

We believe people are looking for leaders who can *shape* the future but not get stuck in their own definitions and visions (*ego intelligence*). They also want leaders who can see and *tune into* opportunities beyond the ordinary and delight them with extraordinary ideas (*intuitive intelligence*). And they look for leaders who can listen to and *integrate* other peoples' thoughts and ideas, valuing everyone's contribution (*eco intelligence*).

Why *intelligence*? For us (the authors) intelligence refers to our sense-making ability or ability to create meaning and solve problems. We as humans do this differently to other mammals, machines and AI. Our intelligence is impacted by our ego needs and emotions, by our identification with the bigger ecosystems we belong to and the quantum world of which we are part. As humans, we are able to identify and connect with three fundamental ways of making sense of the world which we translate into and link to the three forms of intelligence.

First, our *ego intelligence*.

The ego shapes our sense of unique identity, boundaries, ethics and separation in the world or workplace (who I am as separate from you).

Our ego includes our self-esteem or self-importance. Many see the ego as selfish; however, our research found that a mature ego (when we are self-aware and able to manage it appropriately) is a good thing.

The ego brings a sense of certainty and right versus wrong, and it enables leaders to set clear boundaries of what to do and how to do it.

This allows them to shape the future and nudge their organisation into action with focus and speed. When used appropriately and constructively in complex organisations, the ego has a valuable role to play in bringing a single-mindedness for shaping the future, overcoming obstacles and 'making things happen.' We refer to leaders strong in ego intelligence as *Shapers*.

Second, our *intuitive intelligence.* This allows leaders to reach beyond their experience and default programmes into the unseen, non-rational, non-material realm which enables them to see new ways of solving problems. As Steve Jobs[6] said, "Some people say, 'Give the customers what they want.' But that's not my approach. Our job is to figure out (*sense*) what they're going to want before they do."

Intuitive solutions are not based on past data: they bring fresh insights based on non-linear thinking. It is a way of taking unexpected information and feeding our analytical and rational thinking with subtle creative perceptions and new ideas.

Intuition manifests itself as non-rational deep knowing, in our dreams, as flashes of insight or gut feelings that are often fresh and surprising.

The more uncertain the world of work becomes, the more leaders need to develop their own intuition, and make room for intuitive abilities of others in their organisations. It is directly linked to entrepreneurship, courage and risk taking in an organisation. Intuition enables leaders to 'sense into' a situation and know what is needed, but more importantly, 'sensing beyond' the boundaries of a situation to bring fresh perspectives and insights, and connecting the dots in new and innovative ways. We refer to leaders with a strong intuitive intelligence as *Sensors*.

Third, our *eco intelligence.* This is the ability to see ourselves in relation to and connected with others within our ecosystem – for example, leaders feeling a strong resonance and identity with the entire organisational ecosystem or planetary concerns versus their own ego needs. They have the ability to work between and across boundaries.

They apply 'matrix' or 'integrative' thinking which are the abilities to extract value from diverse ideas or models presented by diverse groups of people and technologies.

They can leverage the interdependencies to create something new from existing and often opposing ideas. They create the necessary freedom and psychological safety to stimulate honest and generative dialogue and the emergence of new thinking between stakeholders – in other words, the capacity to 'allow things to happen.' We refer to leaders strong in eco intelligence leaders as *Integrators*.

Agility is key

Way back in 2010, the IBM report[7] Capitalizing on Complexity highlighted that leaders need to be able to deal with complexity and change continuously: they need to be agile and swift. Creativity was identified as the single most important capability. The McKinsey report of 2017[8] 'Jobs Lost, Jobs Gained, Workforce Transitions in a Time of Automation' once again highlighted the need for agility. It pointed out that agility involves being dynamic *and* stable simultaneously. This implies holding a paradox, something that leaders with an 'either-or' mindset find difficult. The McKinsey report confirmed that leaders and organisational units which had embraced agile ways of functioning significantly outperformed other non-agile units on a significant number of criteria.

Our research found that the three intelligences are like interdependent strands of DNA. We suggest that effective agile leadership is a healthy integration of the three intelligences, bringing coherence between them without diluting each one's contribution. Organisations require all three for different reasons and in different contexts.

The key to success lies in the leader's ability to know what is called for 'in the moment' and then being agile enough to bring the most appropriate form of leadership.

This need for a leadership blend within an organisation highlights the importance of distributed or shared leadership. Rather than expecting a single leader to have equally strong ego, eco and intuitive capabilities, it may be more realistic to allow leaders to stay true to themselves within their stage of development and then to ensure that all three capabilities are contained within the leadership team as a whole unit.

But how does the journey to such agility unfold? What development process might an individual or organisation embark on in order to make the most of the three intelligences?

Can caterpillars fly? A journey of personal transformation

We liken the development of a leader (in the nicest possible way!) to that of a caterpillar transforming itself into a butterfly.

Metaphorically, if one asked a caterpillar to fly, it may imagine putting wings onto its little fat body. Flying, however, involves a lot more than adding some wings - it requires a process of transformation.

Figure 1.1

Leaders must be willing to accept the inevitable discomfort (and rewards) of a journey of profound learning – because learning and transformation are synonymous with leading.

Inside a caterpillar there are cells that biologists call 'imaginal cells.' These cells carry the DNA of the butterfly. They are regarded as enemies of the status quo: the caterpillar's immune system fights them. They contain the DNA of the butterfly and carry a new message which they start sharing with each other. This culminates in the imaginal cells clumping together. They start to self-organise into clusters that contain the genes of the different parts of the butterfly. As the caterpillar's immune system fails to overpower them, they grow inside the chrysalis to become a butterfly.

In every person and every organisation, we find imaginal cells containing new ways of thinking and working. At an organisational level, they may initially be regarded with amusement or suspicion, but if they keep growing, the organisation's immune system will fight them. This prevents organisational transformation – it is the antithesis of agility. The same is true for the individual.

Leaders make choices. Some hold on to the recipes of the past success in order to preserve and protect their organisation from intruders that are misaligned with 'the way we do things around here.' Some try to pacify the imaginal cells, suggesting we should try to fly by adding some of their ideas as 'wings' to the current structures. When the wings cannot lift the body, they say, 'I told you it would never work!' Other leaders may consider the new ideas with genuine curiosity and wisdom, exploring the value of the imaginal cells and allowing them to clump and cluster. They monitor their growth, and when the time is right, they have the courage to release the past and embrace a new way: allowing the wings to come from within, to restructure the feet and the body and all the other organs required to relate to the world.

This is also true in individuals. We all need to be open to challenge our own assumptions and beliefs in order to learn, develop and transform ourselves. Fear, arrogance and an absence of curiosity stop us learning fully. 'Busyness' is a great way to avoid asking ourselves challenging questions that could lead to greater self-understanding.

Some leaders are suspicious, some are curious. Some cling to the past, while others let the future emerge through a process of co-creation. Some hold their power tightly through command and control. Some empower others, enabling those around them to be creative and express themselves within the context of their organisation. What kind of leader are you?

This book is about switching on the imaginal cells in leaders and their teams.

It is for those who dream of something bigger: who want to thrive rather than survive in their organisations immune systems.

Notes

1 Zuboff, S. (2019) The Age of Surveillance Capitalism, *Profile Books Ltd*, London.
2 Putin, V. (2017) The Verge, *Vox Publishing LLC*, https://www.theverge.com/2017/9/4/16251226/russia-ai-putin-rule-the-world

   "Artificial intelligence is the future, not only for Russia, but for all humankind," said Putin, reports RT. "It comes with colossal opportunities, but also threats that are difficult to predict. Whoever becomes the leader in this sphere will become the ruler of the world."

3 Schaub, K. (2017) The Fourth Industrial Revolution, *Blackwell*, Hoboken, NJ.
4 Hutchins, G. and Storm, L. (2019) Regenerative Leadership, *Wordzworth*, Tunbridge Wells.
5 Einstein, Albert (1969) The Journal of Transpersonal Psychology, *Association of Transpersonal Psychology*, Palo Alto, CA, Vols. 1–4, p. 124.

   The world that we have made as a result of the level of thinking we have done thus far creates problems that we cannot solve at the same level as the level we created them at.

6 https://www.goodreads.com/quotes/988332-some-people-say-give-the-customers-what-they-want-but
7 IBM report (2010) Capitalizing on Complexity, *IBM Global Business Services*, Somers, NY, https://www.ibm.com/downloads/cas/1VZV5X8J

8 McKinsey & Company Report Jobs lost, jobs gained (November 2017): What the future of work will mean for jobs, skills, and wages. Retrieved from https://www.mckinsey.com/featured-insights/future-of-work/jobs-lost-jobs-gained-what-the-future-of-work-will-mean-for-jobs-skills-and-wages

Chapter 2

Rethinking leadership: some theoretical underpinning

Agility comes as we develop the ability to deal with incompatibility

Theoretical foundations

In this chapter we explore the theoretical foundations of a new leadership logic. We draw on complexity thinking, the concept of human intelligence and the hemispheric structure of the brain. We explain why we believe that truly agile leadership lies in the inter-dependent relationship between ego, eco and intuitive intelligence.

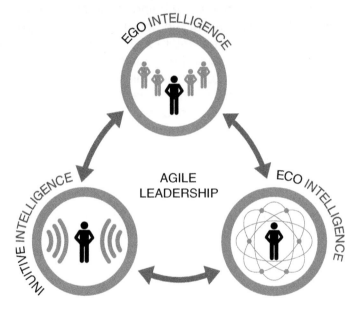

Figure 2.1 The interdependent relationship between ego, eco and intuitive intelligence required for agile leadership

The chapter begins with a look at the evolution of leadership over the last 100 years, examining the underlying assumptions at each stage. It then introduces complexity thinking which under-pins how we understand organisations as self-adapting, living ecosystems. It outlines five fundamental challenges to leadership thinking, explored from a complexity mindset, and introduces the framework we propose as a new leadership logic. It answers the question, 'Why ego, eco and intuitive "intelligence"?' and explains why we have used Robert Dilts'[1] Logical Levels Model to explore behaviour, values, beliefs, and identity in the context of the three intelligences.

Understanding organisations as complex, living ecosystems

The need for a different logic or narrative for organisations and leadership became apparent towards the end of the twentieth century. In the early part of the twentieth century, the rationale for the leader of an organisation was based on the 'scientific' logic of Frederick Taylor (1911)[2] and Henri Fayol (1916)[3]. With the first and second industrial revolutions in full swing, organisations were understood as machines with the leader's role being to direct, to organise and to optimise. In the latter part of the century, this developed into a view which was more dynamic and more demanding – the leader as transforming hero. The logic of the organisation as a machine was still largely in place but the leader became somehow superordinate. He or she had to dominate the machine, force it to change direction through some superhuman capacity which was a combination of inspiration and perspiration. The underlying assumption in this model is that leaders intervene from the 'outside-in' to fix or to change the organisational machine.

At the turn of the twenty-first century this was challenged. Joseph L Badaracco (2001)[4] wrote an article entitled 'We Don't Need Another Hero' in the Harvard Business Review. Heifetz and Laurie (1997)[5] had published a seminal paper extolling a similar message a few years earlier. Many other authors started to share similar views. Not because they did not like the heroic model but because they felt the approach was unrealistic.

Organisational development specialists had long been talking about the need to consider organisations as living systems while some people, including Ralph Stacey (2000)[6], began to offer a view of organisations based on complexity theory. This required an even deeper rethink of the role and nature of leadership. This trend has continued to the present. In the past couple of years alone, a number of highly successful books and articles have talked about toxicity of the heroic, ego-led leader and the need for more shared and self-directed models of leadership where leaders realise that they are part of and not external to the organisation as a living system.

Giles Hutchins and Laura Storm (2019)[7] illustrate this in their book Regenerative Leadership, "The organisation is constantly in dialogue with all of its stakeholders, just as a living organism is constantly sensing, adapting and evolving, within its ecosystem." They go on to say: "… every inter-relation becomes an opportunity to seek deeper authenticity and wholeness through sensing and responding with compassion, courage and vulnerability." This narrative is a long way from many earlier leadership approaches.

Within this context, we were interested in exploring how leaders make sense of the very different world of work in which we find ourselves today. And to delve into how they experienced the process of leading.

Riding the elephant

We asked a number of leaders on our programmes at Hult Ashridge Executive Education to describe what it feels like to lead in their organisation. One leader responded:

> It feels like riding an elephant – I am desperately trying to get this elephant to move in a particular direction but it has a mind of its own and it goes wherever it wants to, leaving me feeling out of control and hanging on for dear life!

Leaders might well be 'in charge' but are they 'in control'?

Does this feel familiar to you?

When Peter Drucker (2009)[8] says, "The greatest danger in times of turbulence, is not the turbulence itself, but to act with yesterday's logic" he is warning leaders not to see the world as predictable and rational. If we view the world as predictable and rational, we will see an organisation like a well-oiled machine, where a leader can be sure that if he/she pushes certain buttons and pulls certain levers, he/she will get certain results. This view implies that formulas exist on how to manage, so managers will continuously look outside for 'best practice' – the tried and tested 'six steps' to achieve staff engagement or the 'five steps' to strategy development, guaranteed to deliver results and provide a sense of achievement and control!

A central theme of this book is the full acceptance of the world as complex and unpredictable – a bit like riding an elephant. This acceptance means that we need to revisit the principles of leadership. Complexity thinking is an interdisciplinary theory that grew out of chaos theory in the 1960s. It draws from research in the natural sciences and quantum mechanics that examines uncertainty and non-linearity. At its roots, complexity thinking assumes that the world is comprised of many elements that interact in an organic way. Many of these elements are unique but adaptable as a result of their interaction with other elements.

When parts interact with each other in a linear, cause and effect way we talk about a *complicated* system, like a machine. The parts in a machine, like a motor car, are complicated but can always be fixed or replaced. There is always a clear solution, the problem can be fixed through some external intervention because there is a clear blueprint of where each part fits and how it should function. In a *complex* system like the human body, nature, families and organisations, the parts (or people) are continually influenced by how they adapt to each other, sometimes fast, sometimes slow. As the parts adapt and change, new ideas or behaviours emerge, the system fixes itself from the inside out. Complex systems are unpredictable and messy and require a different mindset and approach.

Complexity thinking is also based on the concept of *holism,* where the world is not only viewed as a complex system with many parts interacting with each other, but also on the whole entity which is greater than the sum of the parts. All parts of a whole are in intimate interconnection such that they cannot exist independently of the whole or cannot be understood without reference to the whole.

This 'whole' could also relate to the quantum world that exists beyond time and space, a non-material world of 'no-thingness', of pure energy and unlimited possibilities. A world where separation is viewed as an 'illusion' as Hutchins (2014)[9] puts it, because everything is part of the bigger whole. It is a world of pure flow of energy and potential. We are reminded of the butterfly effect[10] in this regard. Many people have an awareness of this world or state of being but ignore it because they cannot find words and formulas to define it. Yet it ultimately directs our lives.

A complexity mindset

A new mindset is required – one which involves the acceptance of the world as complex and unpredictable and views leadership in a fundamentally different way. Seeing organisations as living eco-systems, rather than machines, enables us to embrace the multiple interactions and accompanying feedback loops that constantly change systems and behaviours.

These ecosystems exist in our organisations, whether we like them or not, and whether we are aware of them or not! People learn from, change and adapt in relation to each other continuously. The col-lective attitudes and behaviours in one part of the organisation may influence attitudes and behaviours in related parts and before you know it, something new and surprising has emerged. People talk about it in corridors and on social media. It might be a new behav-iour or attitude towards something in the organisation which the formal communication mechanisms are not capturing because they were designed for a mechanical, command and control system.

This emergence of unpredicted ideas and unexpected behaviour is often triggered by the informal influencers and leaders at any level in an organisation, as seen in the business example below. This can feel quite different to the planned, top-down change envisaged by a senior leader – hence the "riding an elephant" metaphor.

We worked with a large petrochemical organisation to de-velop 287 career ladders and competency profiles for all ma-jor careers – all written at five levels of proficiency. The goal was to enable leaders to conduct more professional, online, competency evaluations of their staff, against these profiles. It was an HR dream come true! Every job profile was defined in detail and put into the large ERP (enterprise resource plan-ning) system. The project was expensive and took two years to complete.

When the time came for the system to 'go live', a few influential senior leaders tried it out. They soon decided that they were not going to use it because it was "far too complicated" and "another HR project...we already have 32 others to deal with!" These senior leaders started talking about it informally among themselves and influenced their peers in management meetings. Within a couple of months, the system had been rejected by most of the senior leadership team as 'another impractical HR system'. What happened next was interesting. Two leaders from Engineering shared that they had developed a much simpler competency system on an Excel spreadsheet a few years earlier – and it was working well for them. Within a month most of the senior leadership team took it upon themselves to tweak and adopt this system from Engineering for their own divisions – at zero additional cost to the organisation. The ERP system was discarded, and the organisation reverted to the simple spreadsheets that the Engineering leaders had proposed. This is a great example of how the informal organisational ecosystem self-organises, and how imposing an intervention rooted in a top down ego-mindset mentality can backfire.

Social media fuels ecosystems

The twentieth century's emphasis on freedom of expression and human rights, supercharged by twenty-first century social media, has had a huge impact on organisations as ecosystems. Individual views and ideas are now easily expressed within organisations via social media platforms and organisational intranets like Facebook, Microsoft Teams or Yammer. As these views are expressed and resonate with many other people, they can create often surprising social movements or pockets of energy for certain ideas or projects. They also enable leaders to keep a more accurate finger on the pulse of the organisational climate or mood. For example, IBM CHRO Diane Gherson[11] explains how they developed a new policy on the use of Uber at IBM. She was able to receive feedback from hundreds of staff all over the world within a couple of hours via their intranet. She was able to respond to them and make some amendments immediately, rather than wait twelve months for the annual engagement survey for disgruntled staff to express their concerns.

What does a complexity mindset mean for organisations?

We suggest that five fundamental shifts are taking place in the world. These will have (and are already having) a profound effect. They highlight the need for a new narrative for leadership. They form the basis of our thinking in this book.

1. From organisations as mechanical systems to organisations as living ecosystems

As we have already mentioned, a classical view of an organisation is synonymous to that of a well-oiled machine (a mindset formed during the first Industrial Revolution), in which human resources can be controlled with clearly defined roles and job descriptions and moved around like pieces on a chessboard. This linear approach (cause and effect) assumes that if I do A, then B will result.

Running organisations as if they were machines often results in a lack of agility and speed due to a reliance on central controlling agents (management) who make decisions at some remote location within a hierarchy.

This may be suitable for military manoeuvres or state-centric models but is profoundly outdated within the modern organisation.

Ralph Stacey's (2000)[12] description of an organisation as a *network of human relationships* is apt because the way in which the future unfolds is affected not only by the complex combinations of rational arguments and influence from informal leaders (as seen in the example above) but also by the emotional reactions, gut feelings, chance, experimentation and opportunism of everyone in the system. With the introduction of cognitive computing and AI, these web-based relationships extend beyond human to human relationships. Up until now, machines were 'dead' in that they had no intrinsic capability for self-learning (smart machines) and adaptability. Today machines enabled by AI are influencing and adapting all the time. We thus have an interplay between the social system, nature (often referred to as the natural ecosystem) and cognitive computing or machine learning. This is why we suggest that leading organisations as ecosystems requires more than emotional intelligence, it also requires the ability to tune in with non-emotional systems based on AI. More about this later.

2. From an 'either-or' to a 'both-and' mindset

A complexity mindset is a 'both-and' mindset in that it can embrace the world as predictable, controllable and linear *and* as chaotic, unpredictable and non-linear. Sometimes the formulas of the past work well to create future success, however, sometimes they are completely inappropriate to the new emerging dynamic within the organisation.

Barry Johnson (1996)[13] points out how many of the current trends in business and industry are polarities to manage rather than problems to solve. For example, it is currently popular to move:

- From neglect of the customer to focusing on the customer
- From individual to team
- From competition to collaboration
- From centralisation to decentralisation
- From rigid structures to flexible arrangements
- From autocratic management to participatory management

Because of a linear approach to change, people tend to define the problem as what we are going 'from' and the solution as what we are going 'to': e.g., to move from *the problem* of centralisation to *the solution* which is decentralisation. This is the limitation we refer to in the next section as blueprint thinking, changing one blueprint for another. However there is a different way of approaching things. Johnson suggests that these trends are better understood as polarities to manage than problems to solve.

Polarities are sets of seeming opposites which cannot function well independently because the two sides of the polarity are interdependent: you cannot choose one as solution and neglect the other, but need 'both-and'.

The objective of a 'both-and' mindset and polarity management is to get the best of both opposites while avoiding the downside of overdoing either of them. For example, the underlying polarity in the centralisation-decentralisation debate is about control vs. empowerment. A 'both-and' mindset will explore how we might achieve control *and* empowerment throughout the organisation.

3. *From blueprint thinking to process thinking*

In the twentieth century it became customary to develop visions for organisations. Most organisational change programmes started with a clear definition of the 'desired future state'. Most leaders assumed their task was to define a compelling vision which often culminated in a blueprint for the future. A linear change process was then designed to mobilise resources and people to 'make it happen'. Blueprint thinking works well in a relatively stable environment where leaders have genuine control over the outcome. The impact of blueprint thinking is that it gives people a sense of destiny and security about the future.

But what if the disruption in the environment becomes so intense that one cannot even begin to define the desired future state?

In times of high uncertainty and low predictability, leaders need to focus more on the journey or process rather than the destination.

The IBM report Capitalizing on Complexity (2010)[14] shows how this journey and process includes creativity and co-creation of services and products.

We are not suggesting that blueprints are bad, as we will show later. An important contribution of ego intelligence is to define outcomes, and there is most definitely a place for it. However, as a business leader from Japan said in the IBM report Capitalizing on Complexity (2010) "in the complex environment we live in, a business model is not an absolute".

CEOs must be able to test and tweak and continuously redesign their core activities. They need to understand how complexity thinking works! They need to constantly have their intuitive antennae out to pick up clues for innovation, to collaborate and be agile to make swift decisions. As a business leader said in the same report, "I sometimes need to change direction 180 degrees after a lunch meeting, so I need my company to be agile enough to deal with this."

Most importantly, they need to be able to release some control to allow and enable the organisation to self-manage, adapt and respond, as it does naturally anyway.

4. *From emotional intelligence to eco intelligence*

Emotional intelligence (EQ) came as a significant breakthrough in the 1990s. Leaders and managers, schoolteachers and parents all embraced this new intelligence. It brought an awareness that people were no longer just human resources, but human beings with strengths and potential... and emotions. Together with the humanistic values of the twentieth century, it contributed to a golden age of humanity in the workplace. As EQ rose in importance, leaders had to develop their 'soft skills' to unlock the emotional capital in the workplace. It brought with it a richness in organisational development and we saw prolific research on people motivation, engagement, inspiring and empathetic leadership. Many leadership programmes still include these themes, and correctly so, as managing self and relationships is still a critical part of leadership effectiveness in the new world of work.

However, we are witnessing a significant move towards a complexity mindset and the realisation of organisations as complex, adaptive ecosystems. This phenomenon is not only seen in human ecosystems but also within the algorithms developed by companies like Google, Apple and YouTube. Their built-in AI picks up our 'clicks', adapts to our preferences and then feeds us advertisements and suggestions of videos to watch or articles to read. The system reads us, feeds us and leads us subtly in many directions. We are also seeing the rise of blockchain (distributed ledger) technologies which are built on complexity thinking principles of: no central controlling agent, self-regulation and transparency.

Futurist Gerd Leonhard (2016)[15] speaks about "humarithms" (as opposed to algorithms); the importance of redefining what it means to be human within a technologically augmented workforce. He points out that the qualities that make us uniquely human like foresight, imagination, curiosity, intuition, love and compassion cannot be nailed down into the 0s and 1s of algorithmic logic. As artificial intelligence takes on much of the left-brain logical thinking and data-orientated jobs, we as humans, are being called upon to bring more of our right-brain, uniquely human qualities to the new world of work. Many recruitment adverts today reflect this, asking for these particular right-brain qualities or humarithms.

For leaders to embrace a complexity mindset within the technologically augmented world of work, they need to recognise a world of both human and artificial intelligence.

Emotional intelligence is of little use when we need to include Sophia the humanoid into the delivery mechanisms of the new world of work, despite the 60 emotions of which she claims to be capable.

So eco intelligence includes and expands beyond emotional intelligence. The eco intelligent leader uses her emotional skills to tune into the needs of people, to understand and motivate, to engage and get commitment. She now needs to add the cognitive skills of integrative thinking and polarity management: to relate and integrate diverse ideas and thoughts of stakeholders, consisting of both the human and artificially intelligent resources. She requires an understanding of how complex adaptive processes work and an ability to leverage the interdependencies effectively, which may often appear as opposing or paradoxical.

5. *From leader to leadership*

Western (2008)[16] points out that whilst leadership is everywhere, the leadership espoused is unattainable to most as it is an elitist, individualised and idealised position at the top of organisations. We suggest that not only is such singularity unattainable but also ineffective, as this view of leadership makes it increasingly difficult to achieve the responsiveness needed to thrive as a twenty-first century organisation.

We are noticing a shift away from pyramid or hierarchical thinking (Figure 2.2) with the leader at the top, to networks (Figure 2.3) where leadership is embedded in a complex web of human and non-human relationships. This shifts the focus from the individual leader towards a recognition that the leadership space is occupied by different people and intelligent robots who step up when the occasion demands.

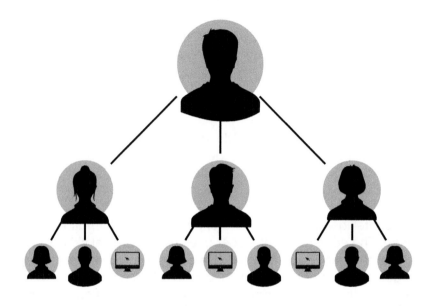

Figure 2.2 Hierarchical pyramid structure

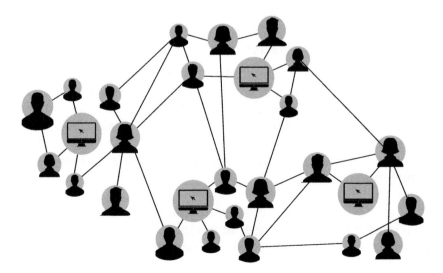

Figure 2.3 Networked organisation

Imagine an organisation where the formal and informal leaders work alongside each other, co-sensing and co-creating the future. If you identify these informal influencers and are able to work with them to co-create and naturally co-live the behaviours and changes you want to see in your organisation, you have an effective way to leverage the natural ecosystem to bring about change. Organisational Network Analysis (ONA) tools are increasingly used to identify the nature of relationships as well as how informal leadership is embedded in the organisation.

Below is an example of how Bâloise (a European insurance organisation) leveraged the power of their informal influences by starting with an ONA:

Viral change via 'sparks'

The senior team realised the importance of leveraging their informal leaders who they knew were distributed across the organisation at all levels. They conducted an ONA survey with all 7,000 employees asking two simple questions, 'Who in Bâloise are you most likely to listen to? 'Who in Bâloise are you most likely to be influenced by?'

Three hundred informal influencers/leaders were identified and fondly named 'sparks.' These sparks were approached and invited to form a community to participate in bringing about 'viral' change (very naturally getting others to catch the virus of new ways of behaving). They were empowered to do what they felt was needed to bring about the change of culture. These sparks have since become an integral and important part of the journey. They simply live the new behaviours in all their interactions and are trusted by the senior leaders to do what they feel is needed.

For example – one of the changes envisaged was to create a more 'human' and informal climate. One morning, some of the sparks planned to run a short survey during breakfast in the staff dining hall, asking all staff and leaders whether they wanted to change the way staff and leaders address each other from the polite, formal German 'Sie' (you) to the informal 'du' (you). Eighty-five percent voted to change to the more informal language, and from that day onwards the sparks simply started using this new language, and it soon became the norm throughout the organisation. A more comprehensive exposition of the Bâloise story is offered in Chapter 7, on page 185.

Why do we use the word leadership 'intelligence'?

The American Psychological Association defines intelligence as 'the ability to derive information, learn from experience, adapt to the environment, understand, and correctly utilise thought and reason'[17]. However, there are numerous other definitions of intelligence. The debate about defining intelligence has been ongoing since the French psychologist Alfred Binet[18] developed his intelligence test as early as 1905. Since then we have seen many intelligence tests and many debates on what intelligence is and how to measure it. Howard Gardner[19] challenged the 'conventional' concept of intelligence in the 1980s and introduced nine intelligences.

As mentioned earlier, the 1990s saw the emergence of 'emotional intelligence', popularised by the work of Daniel Goleman (1995)[20]. In (2000)[21] Danah Zohar and Ian Marshall wrote their ground-breaking work on 'spiritual intelligence'. Apart from giving intelligence a neurological basis, they showed how developing our Spiritual Quotient (SQ) will help us to deal with the complexity of the new world of work. We owe some of our thinking to this and their subsequent work.

Our own thinking on human intelligence finds its roots in the social constructivist work of Berger and Luckmann (1966)[22]. Both were guest lecturers at the University of South Africa (UNISA) in the 1970s when we as sociologists[23] were trying to find a way of reconstructing a society that was falling apart due to the philosophy and policies of apartheid. They argue that humans are called 'homo sapiens' which means 'the wise one', or the animal that makes plans. While animals rely mostly on their instincts, humans are blessed (or cursed) with intelligence to survive in the world. Within the context of this wisdom we define intelligence as our 'meaning or sense making capability'. For us 'making meaning' includes understanding but also constructing or co-constructing the world we live in.

'Meaning' therefore refers to creating, adopting or shaping our lifeworld according to our human needs and orientation towards life. This existential project is as much an individual as a social one. Unlike some species in the animal world, we are dependent on social interaction to construct our world. The human world is made up of nature but much more, our culture. And culture is the result of how we make meaning. Our upbringing, socialisation process, emotional wounds etc, all impact on how we make sense of things or create our meaning. The three intelligences can be explained as three meaning-making orientations or intelligences as discussed below.

Ego intelligence (the shaper) makes sense of a situation by defining or shaping it. Relying on clear boundaries and definitions, e.g. delineating myself or my team as separate from others. It is our sense of identity, of who we are. Through our ability to define and give names (using language) to things and other people, we start to shape the world according to our needs to define it and make sense of it, and this is how culture emerges.

Intuitive intelligence (the sensor) is knowing without words and definitions. It makes sense or meaning of the world by drawing on the non-rational, e.g., gut feel or heart knowing, and even the quantum realm, tuning into the universal flows and patterns that influence us or the macro forces impinging on our organisations. It senses into a space of unlimited possibilities.

Eco intelligence (the integrator) uses social constructionist logic in making sense of the world by co-creating meaning with others. It is our ability to relate to and integrate diverse ideas, things and people into our world; restoring balance or coherence. Eco intelligence is our ability to reconcile sometimes opposing forces or polarities, to create something new. The arithmetic of eco intelligence is 1+1=3.

This is well illustrated in the working of our human brain.

Intelligence and the structure of the brain

A word of caution before we start this section. We do not claim to be experts in neurology but see a more metaphoric value in this exploration, and we realise that the working of the brain is more complex than the hemispheric interaction.

We are inspired by the ground-breaking work of Iain McGilchrist (2009)[24] on the hemispheric structure of the brain, how the right and left hemispheres function and how they collaborate through the integrative working of the corpus callosum. We draw some parallels between the three intelligences and the structure of the brain. McGilchrist draws parallels between the structure of the brain and how one perceives or constructs (makes sense or meaning) of the world. This resonates with our view of intelligence as our meaning-making mechanism.

McGilchrist points out that mainstream neuroscience has to a large extent stopped referring to the differences between the two hemispheres which were oversimplified during the 1960s and early 1970s. The evidence is that although there are distinct differences between the two hemispheres, the key to successful functioning lies in the interdependencies between the two hemispheres: how they work together but also how they work separately when necessary. The corpus callosum is responsible for the cooperation between them but also inhibits interference between them when the occasion demands it.

The right hemisphere gives sustained, broad, open vigilance and alertness. The right brain looks out for those things that might be beyond the scope of our expectations and attention. It sees the bigger context and understands metaphor, body language and emotional expressions.

The right brain has a sense of wholeness and sees the world as whole, interconnected, and changing, never fully graspable or fully knowable.

Intuitive intelligence draws on the functioning of the right brain.

The left hemisphere on the other hand gives narrow, sharply focused, attention to detail.

We also use the left brain to give names to things and people, using language to fit them into a predefined framework. It gives us a simplified version of reality and filters out a lot of information. It is dependent on language, abstraction and brings clarity which enables us to manipulate things that are fixed and known. People who lose their right hemisphere (through an accident or surgery) have a pathological narrowing of the window of attention. Ego intelligence draws on the functioning of the left brain.

The two hemispheres give us two different ways of interpreting reality which leaves us with a sense of a paradoxical reality.

This is where the role of the corpus callosum becomes very interesting because of the 'collaborative' role it plays (with other subcortical structures) between the two hemispheres.

McGilchrist argues that for people to function well, the two hemispheres need to share information but at the same time to keep the way that information is handled, separate.

This facilitative capability of the corpus callosum is in line with our understanding of eco intelligence. While it recognises the independence of the two hemispheres it leverages the hemispheric interdependencies and creates a space of emergence. When the two hemispheres are surgically divided and the corpus callosum becomes inactive, people have extraordinary experiences. One man reported that with one arm he was embracing his wife while pushing her away with the other. A woman reported that she had to stop driving, because her left hand was trying to drag the right hand off the steering wheel. These examples provide good metaphors for some of the conflicts in organisations where eco intelligence is absent!

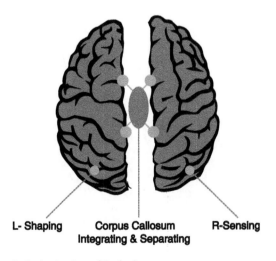

L- Shaping   **Corpus Callosum**   R-Sensing
Integrating & Separating

Figure 2.4 The hemispheric structure of the brain

If the whole brain is not working in a coherent way the body suffers, and it impacts on our relationships with others. Hence our emphasis on the collaboration between the three intelligences. Coherence and interaction are critical to enable the different intelligences to work together. Their full potential can only be realised in this coherence. As we will see later, when the paradoxical relationship between the three intelligences is lost, we see their downsides.

Understanding the depth of the transformational journey

We realise that in order to understand leadership behaviour more fully, we need to dive below the waterline. In our research we used the Logical Levels model of Robert Dilts (1988)[25] to explore the underlying (below the waterline) drivers of human behaviour within the framework of ego, eco and intuitive leadership.

Commonly referred to as the Iceberg Framework, it offers a hierarchy of below-the-water-line processes within an individual or group that need to be recognised and addressed for behaviour to be understood or changed. In the Appendix, we share our research findings on all of the levels described below for each of the three intelligences.

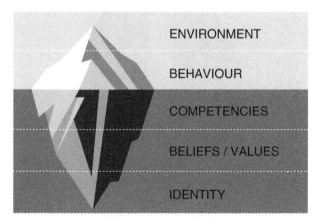

Figure 2.5 Robert Dilts' logical levels depicted within the Iceberg Framework

The various levels can be described as follows:

Levels 1 & 2 environment and behaviour

These are the observable, visible 'above the waterline' elements of the model. Environment is about the external conditions in which behaviour takes place. It refers to the questions where and when? As discussed in Chapter 1, many leaders experience the environment today as turbulent. The environmental conditions trigger certain behaviours: people can either react (impetuously) to these stimuli from the environment or they respond (thoughtfully) to these in terms of the 'below the waterline' levels.

For the purpose of our research we have combined levels 1 & 2 Environment and Behaviours.

Level 3 competence

The focus of this level is, 'what abilities do leaders possess?' It provides an answer to the question, 'how we do what we do'. What skills and competencies are required? Each of the three intelligences provides a certain cluster of competences to enable leaders to respond to situations.

Level 4 beliefs and values

In order to simplify questions in our research we combined beliefs and values. On this level we consider 'why we do what we do'. Leaders in a similar situation may respond differently depending on their values and beliefs. These beliefs may be empowering or disempowering, they could reinforce or undermine their ability to act.

Level 5 identity

This refers to the question of 'who am I?' or my sense of self. Conversations on this level refer to one's level of self-actualisation and one's perception of self, e.g., 'I the visionary', or 'I am the servant leader'. We used metaphors to help leaders identify these by asking questions like 'When I am leading at my best, I am like a...?'

Changing something on a lower level will radiate upward, pre-cipitating change on the upper levels. Changing something on an upper level (e.g., behaviour) could, but would not necessarily, affect the lower levels.

Agile leadership as a process

As indicated in the spiral diagram below, leadership can be viewed as a process of divergence, convergence and emergence over time. The process of *divergence* opens up the space for creative and intuitive insights or ideas from diverse stakeholders to be born, heard and considered with an open mind. This process leads to the *emergence* of new thinking and new ideas that need to be taken to some conclusion or not. This is where ego intelligence becomes important with its ability to bring *convergence:* shaping the out-come into something tangible and then driving it to a conclusion. Through the process of implementing actions over time; obstacles, ideas, learnings will continue to emerge, which then again are taken into the creative divergent space for consideration, brainstorming and intuitive insights. It is an iterative process. A version of this spiral 'the double diamond' is often used in design thinking to drive innovation in organisations.

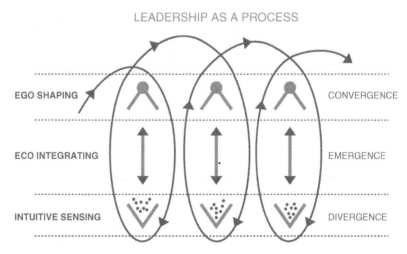

Figure 2.6 Spiral diagram depicting leadership as a process

Eco intelligence comes into play by creating the right conditions and psychological safety for this iterative process of divergence, convergence and emergence to happen, in other words for the organisational ecosystem to flourish. Our eco intelligence helps us to continuously *integrate* the fixed definitions of things, ideas and structures of the ego with the new and fresh thinking of the intuition.

This chapter in a nutshell

We live in a world today that is characterised by turbulence, ambiguity and uncertainty. It has become increasingly challenging for single leaders to 'know the future' and to 'know the way' and to manage the organisation like a well-oiled machine – in fact it often feels more like 'riding an elephant'.

Complexity thinking offers a different way of seeing the organisation as a network of relationships or as a living ecosystem, constantly influenced and affected by a complex and unpredictable combination of factors.

A complexity mindset is able to embrace the world as predictable, controllable and linear *as well as* chaotic, unpredictable and non-linear.

Five important shifts are indicative of a complexity mindset:

- From organisation as mechanical system to organisation as living ecosystem
- From either-or mindset to a both-and mindset
- From blueprint thinking to process thinking
- From emotional intelligence to eco intelligence
- From leader to leadership

Leadership is a process that involves the integration of divergence, convergence and emergence, within which the three intelligence each have a crucial and interdependent role to play. Understanding the three intelligences can be enriched through the metaphor of the structure of the human brain: left brain *ego,* right brain *intuitive* and corpus callosum *eco* intelligence.

In order to grow and expand their leadership repertoire, leaders are encouraged to delve below the waterline of the iceberg and undergo a journey of personal reflection and development to ensure they understand the assumptions and beliefs that drive their behaviour. Chapter 6 explores the personal development journey in greater depth.

Reflection and application

- Do you think the world needs a new kind of leadership during these turbulent times? Why do you say so? What kind of leadership do you feel is needed?

- When you think of the word "organisation" what image comes to mind?

- How would you say your image represents your view of the organisations? For example, a complex, living ecosystem, a well-oiled machine, networks of relationships, a physical place, a family of colleagues and friends?

- How does this view of an organisation influence 'how' you lead your team?

- How has your organisation been impacted by technology, AI and the push towards data driven decision making?

- Which of the three intelligences is your strength and which is your development area? Why do you say so?

Notes

1 Dilts, Robert B. (2014) A brief history of logical levels, http://www.nlpu.com/Articles/LevelsSummary.htm
2 Taylor, F. (1911) The Principles of Scientific Management, *Harper & Bros*, New York.

3 Fayol, H. (1916) Administration Industrielle et Générale, Bulletin de la *Société de l'Industrie Minérale*, Translated into English by Storr, C. (1949) General and Industrial Management, *Sir Isaac Pitman & Sons*, London.
4 Badaracco, J. L. (2001) We don't need another hero, *Harvard Business Review*.
5 Heifetz, R. A. and Laurie, D. L. (1997) The work of leadership, *Harvard Business Review*.
6 Stacey, R. (2000) Complexity and Management, *Routledge*, London.
7 Hutchins, G. and Storm, L. (2019) Regenerative Leadership, *Wordzworth*, Tunbridge Wells.
8 Drucker, P. (2009) quoted in Neharika, V. and Kumar, M., The relevance of Peter Drucker's work: Celebrating Drucker's 100th birthday, *Vickalapa*.
9 Hutchins, G. (2014) The Illusion of Separation, *Floris Books*, Edinburgh.
10 The theory that small actions can have non-linear effects in complex systems.
   Also the film The Butterfly Effect, Mackye Gruber, J, and Bress, E., BenderSpink, Film Engine and Catalyst Films, 2004.
11 Dianne Gherson mentions this in a talk during the IBM HR Summit: Re-Imagining HR in the Cognitive era: https://www.youtube.com/watch?v=10HB2dsSybE&t=15s
12 Stacey, R. (2000) Complexity and Management, *Routledge*, London.
13 Johnson, B. (1996) Polarity Management, *HRD Press*, Amherst, MA.
14 IBM report (2010) Capitalizing on Complexity, *IBM Global Business Services*, Somers, NY, https://www.ibm.com/downloads/cas/1VZV5X8J
15 Leonhard, G. (2016) Technology v Humanity, *Fast Future Publishing*, New York.
16 Western, S. (2008) Leadership: A Critical Text, *Sage Publications*, London.
17 https://dictionary.apa.org/intelligence.
18 https://www.verywellmind.com/alfred-binet-biography-2795503
19 https://www.britannica.com/biography/Howard-Gardner
20 Goleman, D. (1995) Emotional Intelligence, *Bantam Books*, New York.
21 Zohar, D. and Marshall, I. (2000) Spiritual Intelligence, *Bloomsbury Publishing*, London.
22 Berger, P. L. and Luckmann, T. (1966) The Social Construction of Reality, Anchor Books/Doubleday, Garden City, NY.
23 Frederick was a sociologist at UNISA at that time.
24 McGilchrist, I. (2009) The Master and His Emissary, *Yale University Press*, New Haven, CT.
25 Dilts, Robert B. (2014) A brief history of logical levels, http://www.nlpu.com/Articles/LevelsSummary.htm

Chapter 3

Ego
intelligence:
the shaper

The benevolent ego is a powerful
part of a leader's armoury, but
a stuck ego can become its
greatest enemy

Our ego... friend or foe?

Contemporary leadership literature suggests that ego is unhelpful in a leader, driving negative and corrosive behaviours leading to the disempowerment of others. Leaders like Donald Trump, Elon Musk and Steve Jobs are sometimes described as egotistical, called narcissists and are often criticised for their 'big egos'. Donald Trump appears to act almost completely at the behest of his ego, unable to tolerate the smallest criticism or disagreement. Steve Jobs was fired from his own company due to his 'unmanageable ego![1]' Elon Musk was so incensed by a refusal to use his miniature submarine in a cave rescue in Thailand that he resorted to insulting a respected rescue diver in a widely shared tweet[2]. Can people like this be seen as good leaders?

An internet search for 'ego' and 'leadership' highlights dozens of articles and books saying that leaders should be selfless and 'ego free'. But the ego is an inescapable part of ourselves. To pretend someone is 'ego free' is unrealistic. Rather, we should recognise different stages of ego development and value the important contribution of the benevolent ego in the mature, self-aware leader. In this chapter, we recognise what we call the shadows or downsides of ego but also value the essential gifts and strengths it brings.

Let's look briefly at what we mean by 'ego'.

In general terms, the ego refers to one's self-concept or identity: who 'I' am uniquely and distinctively in the world. It gives us our sense of differentiation. How 'I' relate to and make sense of the world. We, as humans, naturally operate within the safety of individual ego boundaries (me), which can also extend to my team, my organisation, my country or other identity markers such as my culture.

The ego also assigns names and identities to other people and other things to help with its orientation in the world. One could say the ego engages in a 'naming game.' Berger P.L. & Luckmann, T. (1966)[3] call this 'objectivation.' Ideas and experiences get objectified by giving them a name or turning them into an object like a piece of art, a song or a motor car. Once an idea or experience has been objectified, it can be shared with others and start to have a life of its own. This process of naming and objectivation creates diversity and boundaries, resulting in separation between people, communities, organisations, departments, etc. The ego is therefore the author of diversity in the world and more specifically for us, in the workplace. Once the ego has given names to things and people, it has a sense of how to work with them, control them or even manipulate them. Also, because of the ego's attachment to predefined outcomes, it may find it difficult to change and adapt in disruptive situations.

Mindset – a world consisting of parts that can be shaped and directed

In order to 'think clearly', the ego sees the world as consisting of separate elements which can be named and shaped through assembling the different parts. This is a mechanistic view of the world as a system that is held together by means of cause and effect relationships. We describe the ego as the 'manager' or 'shaper' aspect of ourselves. It can be imagined as a rider using the strength of their horse, guiding it in a certain direction. As a sense-making capability, it enables us to think clearly, to analyse and evaluate issues and to make decisions.

The ego gives us a sense that we can shape and control the world to fit our needs and desires. In the workplace this has both positive benefits like clear accountability and control as well as negative implications such as stereotyping and the creation of organisational silos.

Drawing on left brain functioning, the ego brings us focused attention and a narrowing of our experience of reality through rationality and language. This is in contrast with the right brain, which opens up attention and uses imagination, emotion and metaphor to interpret our reality.

Ego intelligence plays a critical role in shaping ideas in the early phases of developing an idea or piece of work, then in refocusing and reshaping at various points on a journey until the concept or project turns into a reality.

We use Steve Jobs and Elon Musk as examples in this and the next chapter on intuitive intelligence, as two of the most successful businessmen in the world who are often praised for their intuitive abilities. The importance of ego in their success should not be underestimated. We believe that it was the ego that gave them their drive and focus. And that it was the ego that shaped their ideas and mobilised people to follow them and make things work.

Ego intelligence and digitalisation

In Chapter 1 we discussed how digital disruption is impacting our world of work. This argument can be taken a step further by considering the use of algorithms and AI as an extension of the left-brain activity. What is the relationship between the human ego and digitalisation?

The left-brain is good at working with and processing data. It is significant that smart machines are outperforming humans when it comes to the gathering and processing of large volumes of data. The use of data and AI amplifies the ego's role of naming and identifying categories of people and things and clarifying cause and effect relationships and trends. Our (provocative) view is that it enhances the ego's ability to manipulate, command and control and contributes to the dehumanisation of the workplace.

This use of data to build patterns about human behaviour to predict future behaviour has to a large extent objectified human behaviour. HR practitioners often pride themselves by saying how data is helping them to recruit more effectively because it minimises the subjective and intuitive aspects of taking decisions about recruitment. It is significant that many companies still refer to the people working for them as (human) resources.

Iain McGilchrist (2009)[4] uses the metaphor of the Master (the right brain) and his Emissary (left brain), arguing that the Emissary, who was supposed to serve the Master and explore the Kingdom, actually hijacked the kingdom, creating fragmentation. Is this what is happening in the world of work with AI? Is the ability to process huge amounts of data logically and rationally determining how we consider everything – denying us the ability to use all our human intelligences, in the broadest sense, to explore situations and make sense of things?

The benevolent ego

The benevolent or liberated ego comes to the fore when we have achieved a degree of maturity and self-awareness. It means that we can use the strengths of our ego, but our behaviour is not dominated or dictated by it. A benevolent ego is less caught up in its needs for security, acceptance and status, and is able to focus on a bigger goal or higher purpose in service to others. Leaders with a benevolent ego are therefore able to more consciously use their ego's strength to achieve results rather than their ego needs controlling or hijacking them, as Sharon shares in the personal story below.

I was raised as the cherished only child with a mother who continuously placed me on a pedestal saying things like "you are an achiever, you stand out, you can achieve anything if you put your mind to it!" Standing out (differentiation) became an ego pattern and I found myself becoming quite dependent on recognition from people, which I realise is the shadow of the ego. I noticed that when I was not placed in the centre stage, I felt rejected. Over time, and with much introspection, I am now able to recognise when I am falling into this ego trap. My self-awareness nowadays enables me to notice when this ego conditioning is at play and I manage to (mostly) put those needs in perspective and to act with humility, and use my ego strengths more consciously, rather than being hijacked by them.

The benevolent ego helps us to be focused *and* creative. When we say creative, the ego is not necessarily the originator of ideas, but it plays an important role in shaping ideas and bringing them to fruition. Original ideas are more the result of intuitive insight (intuitive intelligence) or generative dialogue (eco intelligence). However, objectivation means that ego can turn 'no-thing' into 'some-thing' by giving it a name, thereby creating 'new-things'.

The benevolent ego can therefore work with intuitive and eco intelligence to serve instead of dictate, to take ideas, shape and turn them into something tangible.

Importantly for innovation, the ego can create boundaries, but it can also *cross boundaries*. It can be the explorer of new opportunities, turning them into tangible realities. In the workplace some leaders unleash this creative ability in their staff, encouraging them to explore opportunities across the organisational boundaries rather than caging them in role descriptions, rules and regulations.

The upsides (gifts) of ego intelligence

Because of the negative perceptions of the ego leader, some leaders in our research shied away from developing their ego strengths. So rather than using the ego to play to its strengths (the benevolent ego), they try to adopt an eco style.

We interviewed such a leader during our research. He tried to engage his people in decision making, asking them to define their own jobs, allowing them to self-organise and do all the things that may be expected from an ego-less leader. During the interview he proudly explained how he was doing all the 'people stuff' right. However, when we talked to his team-members they were not happy at all! "He is never there to take decisions when we need him... he always leaves decisions to us ... we have to figure out what to do..." This leader had completely forgotten how to read the context and to use the positive aspects of ego intelligence, e.g., to create the necessary structure with a team who were still in a dependency mode. He could have taken them on a progressive journey towards empowerment rather than moving so quickly from 'providing direction' to 'offering autonomy'. He went to the opposite extreme in order to be seen as an enabling 'hands-off' eco leader which was not the right thing to do for this team at this time. Reading the team and the context is so important.

We summarise the gifts of the benevolent ego to the organisation as capabilities in three categories: 'head' (thinking capabilities), 'heart' (emotional capabilities) and 'hands' (action):

Head: the way the benevolent ego thinks

The ability to name things is rooted in the ego's ability to analyse and break or reduce (reductionism) things into parts. Ego intelligent leaders have a linear way of thinking. They eliminate paradox with clear right-wrong, fit-misfit arguments. They are not good at dealing with opposition because they hold strong views of what is right or wrong and when challenged will tend to cut off or eliminate ideas or people who don't fit with their way. The benefit of this is clarity, focus and speed. This is why ego intelligence operates well when fast convergence on goal directed action is needed. It eliminates or sidelines ideas and people who are not aligned with the outcome or the group, and in the process saves a lot of time and energy. Ego intelligent leaders attract followers who need, and like, direction and focus. They have a specific approach to dealing with emotions.

Heart: the way the ego deals with emotions – identity and emotional safety

Because the ego is our sense of identity, it gives us a sense of orientation and security in knowing who we are and what we want. It also enables us to think clearly about what is right and wrong, good and bad. We feel safe when we are doing the 'right thing' or being 'good'. We want to be recognised and accepted by others and have a need to comply in order to quench this need for belonging.

Ego intelligent leaders create this sense of belonging for those who 'buy-in' to the vision and values, leading to a sense of pride and patriotism, a tribal mindset, excluding those who do not 'fit' or belong to us (in-group and out-group). They develop a sense of safety and security within the boundaries and a ringfencing of the group versus others. Branding, both personal and organisational, is an essential part of identity. An example is Donald Trump's rhetoric during his election campaign in 2015. 'America First' which was aimed at instilling national pride in the 'in-group' while his other key message, 'build the wall' nicely defined the 'out-group'!

In a turbulent world, the need for security and certainty should not be underestimated. There seems to be a tendency that the strong charismatic leader offering certainty often wins against those who show vulnerability and uncertainty.

As we see in politics, people are often prepared to follow leaders promising certainty, even in the face of disturbing facts about the leader. What these leaders promise may well not happen; but their visions of the future are almost like drugs that help people feel a sense of safety and security about the future even if they do not make rational sense.

Ego intelligent leaders are often *persuasive.* They use a combination of thinking and feeling capabilities to influence others. Their primary approach is to use their *own energy* (vs that of others) to build engagement and support. They say things like "it's lonely at the top" or "if it is going to be, it is up to me!"

They influence others through inspirational speeches, convincing arguments and sometimes even the use of fear by ensuring consequences for non-compliance to their ideas. They are often able to deliver a compelling vision and build buy-in of their ambition in the minds of their supporters. While this will include logical elements, some ego leaders are excellent users of rhetoric, imagery, metaphor and other storytelling techniques to engage their followers at an emotional level.

Finally, ego intelligent leaders lead from the front, often with huge passion and conviction.

They determine the vision and brand identity for people to follow. One of the leaders we interviewed during our research had an interesting story about the time that he worked with Henry Kissinger in the US president's office when he was young. Apparently, Kissinger always said that it was not his task to keep the people that worked for him happy and motivated on the contrary, his people should keep him, as the leader, happy and motivated. "The leader is the one who needs to be nurtured and motivated by his people, because if it wasn't for him the business wouldn't exist after all!"

Hands: the benevolent ego in action – 'making things happen'

Perhaps the most powerful capability of ego intelligence is the ability to make things happen. With little fear and low concern for upsetting the apple cart, the ego intelligent leader can drive disruption, create turbulence, make people think and create new things. He/she can respond to opportunities and shape them into tangible, concrete realities.

Ego intelligence gives us the ability to shape our world; to draw organigrams, provide clear job descriptions, develop KPIs, map business processes and fit people into jobs. The ego intelligent leader's edge lies in their ability to do what is needed, in the moment, even if it leads to a negative reaction and short-term unpopularity. This is an essential capability and generates respect amongst followers – even if they may sometimes feel a little bruised.

Competition lies at the heart of the ego leader's drive to make things happen. This refers to the ego's need to grow, to improve itself and to outperform others. Ego intelligent leaders use competitiveness in the workplace to get people to perform better. They look to explore in order to conquer which drives innovation as well as growth, often making a business more competitive and heathier. This operates at every level from a small business looking to grow it's turnover from zero to something meaningful, right through to a nation state looking to expand its geographical influence and control. This logic is often clear and obvious to people and as such can be used as a rallying call and source of motivation. Anyone who questions it may be considered as disloyal or lacking commitment.

This course of action requires courage – a key ingredient in a successful leader. Growth involves risk, rapid growth often involves significant risk.

An ego leader may well be required to come across as strong and confident, the rock that people attach themselves to in a storm. A participant on a programme Colin was running used the vernacular term 'bottle' (English slang for courage or the ability to hold ones' nerve/not panic) to describe a key leadership characteristic.

Sports coaches often reinforce their teams' strength by positioning every other team as 'the enemy'. An example of this happened in top-flight English football in the 1980s and 1990s. An unfashionable Wimbledon FC gatecrashed English football's elite in 1986 having played in the lowest professional tier only four years earlier. Most commentators predicted relegation at the end of their first season. Instead they remained in the top-flight for over a decade, winning the FA cup in 1988, operating on a budget that was a fraction of their competitors. They developed a siege mentality. With the nick-name 'The Crazy Gang' they played a high tempo, physical style of football, revelling in the fact that none of the top teams enjoyed playing against them. The coach, Joe Kinnear, built the identity of the team on the fact that they were 'different', unwelcome outsiders in a closed circle of established top-flight clubs. This gave the players a sense of security, belonging to an 'in group' (Wimbledon FC) that was fighting for its place in a system that did not welcome them.

Some business leaders use this logic internally as well as externally: setting operating divisions or countries in competition with each other to drive up performance for example to become the 'best region', sometimes at the cost of the larger organisational performance or morale.

The downsides (shadows) of ego intelligence

The downside or negative aspects of ego intelligence appear when the ego is trapped in a particular emotional state or in self-centred needs as we will discuss in Chapter 6. This is when the ego gets a bad reputation, when it draws its energy from it's shadow of self-centredness and uses its ego strengths to dictate the way forward.

The downside of the ego shows up because of many reasons, but the following seem to be some of the most obvious.

Ego 'stuckness'

This occurs when a leader's drivers of everyday behaviour are overly influenced by their personal ego needs for security, acceptance or status. They have insufficient self-awareness to recognise, put into perspective and use their ego strengths constructively.

This results in unhelpful behaviours such as blaming others, taking too much credit, playing the system for self-gain and intolerance of criticism.

A stuck ego becomes rigid and persistent. Its emotional charge releases a tremendous amount of energy towards the achievement of goals, quite often because of a 'fear of failure' and attachment to their pre-defined outcomes. These goals may be good and uplifting but the underlying driving force is the ego's need for recognition or acceptance. They appear to be the heroes because they so strongly believe and identify with these outcomes. Their weakness often becomes their 'strength' and they often attract like-minded people to follow them in the pursuit of the lofty ideals.

Overplaying the ego's strengths

Any overplayed strength often becomes a weakness. If ego is the dominant driver of a leader's thinking and behaviour, the interdependent relationship with the other two intelligences breaks down.

An example of overplayed ego is the seemingly relentless pursuit of growth by many large companies in the 1990s. One could argue that this was partly driven by unrealistic expectations of growth in share value by stockholders which could only be achieved through acquisition, not organic growth or operational efficiencies. But it was also driven by the unfettered ego intelligence of some top managers. Royal Bank of Scotland's acquisition of the Dutch Bank ABN in 2007 was the last in a relentless series of acquisitions by NatWest over the previous decade but it was seen by many as an example of the pursuit of growth for growth's sake and led to the demise of CEO Fred Goodwin[5].

In summary, when ego intelligence is driven by unfulfilled ego needs, it deserves the bad publicity it receives. However, when it becomes liberated from these traps and takes on the role of "servant' to intuitive and eco intelligence, its gifts can be incredibly valuable in shaping and forming initiatives in service to the wider community.

In Chapter 6 we delve deeper into the concept of a stuck versus benevolent ego by exploring ego development and the drivers of behaviours we experience at the various life stages. We look at how this influences how we lead. We also provide insights into how to raise self-awareness through our personal development journey towards benevolence and servant leadership.

Under the waterline

For an overview of how these gifts and shadows are underpinned by below the behavioural waterline factors such as values, beliefs and identity, please see the Dilts Logical Levels model in the Appendix.

Developing your ego intelligence

We share some practical suggestions from our research and from participants in the classroom on developing the gifts of ego intelligence.

Head – thinking	Heart – feelings	Hands – action
• Have a clearly articulated vision and strategy for your business or team	• Create a strong feeling of pride/unity/belonging/family/tribe by instilling a clear brand and identity with your team e.g. use of team names, slogans, symbols, rituals	• Take ideas (yours and others) and shape them into tangible actions with clear responsibilities allocated to people

Head – thinking	Heart – feelings	Hands – action
• Set ambitious and clear goals and targets	• Clarify confusing issues so individuals and teams know what is expected of them collectively and individually e.g. create clear role descriptions and team charters	• Be prepared to take a stand and to speak out
• Provide a clear plan to bring the needed focus and convergence to achieve your vision	• Make behavioural boundaries clear to people – which behaviours are acceptable which are not	• Make decisions quickly (even if not 100% clear) and move to action efficiently
• Build team structures, develop processes and clear role definitions that delineate your team from others	• Be persuasive and inspirational to keep you team focused and motivated. Share your ideas clearly and with confidence and conviction	• Create and implement clear strategies of how you intend to 'win' against competition
• Make sure that you are able to speak with knowledge and authority when you communicate with the organisation…be well prepared	• Develop clear processes and structures to get your organisation running like a 'well-oiled machine'	• Monitor and measure progress of initiatives and people performance
• Develop a clear sense of 'who you are' as a leader, 'what you need' and 'what you stand for' (personal brand)	• Ensure positive reinforcement when desired results are achieved. Celebrate achievements when they occur	• Give regular feedback and reward to people for achieving the goals
	• Bring a sense of security to your team by communicating certainty about the future, e.g., that there is a clear plan to deal with uncertainties, and that all is 'in hand'	• Give clear guidance and feedback about your expectations of your team

Head – thinking	Heart – feelings	Hands – action
	• Be a strong example for others to follow – walk the talk	• Conduct analysis of data/ trends in order to stay up to date with important knowledge and facts about the business

This chapter in a nutshell

We believe that the ego is an inescapable part of ourselves: to pretend someone is 'ego free' is unrealistic. The ego refers to one's self-concept or identity: who 'I' am uniquely and distinctively in the world. It gives us our sense of differentiation. The ego also assigns names and identities to other people and other things to help with its orientation in the world. One could say the ego engages in a 'naming game'. This is known as 'objectivation'. We argued that algorithmic thinking and smart machines became good allies to the ego in the way ego intelligence functions.

We point out the value to an organisation of recognising the contribution of a benevolent ego (an ego that is liberated from its stuckness in ego needs), and shared how these gifts can become a weakness (shadows) if they are overplayed or become trapped in unfulfilled eco needs. The benevolent ego brings the gifts of convergence, focus, speed and a sense of identity and emotional security to their teams though certainty and belonging. This is particularly attractive to followers during times of turbulence.

On the shadow side, leaders trapped in their ego needs for security, acceptance or recognition become too attached to 'proving their value' because of their fear of failure or rejection. This can lead to what gives the ego its bad reputation – self-centredness, self-promotion, blaming others and an inability to receive criticism.

Reflection and application

Think about times in your life when you (or a leader close to you) used ego intelligence to bring identity, focus and direction, what was the situation?

- How did ego intelligence manifest in what they/you did and how they/you did it?

- What worked well and what did not work? What was the impact – positive or negative?

- Can you think of times when you have experienced the shadow side of your ego needs – for example, when you were driven by your need for security, acceptance, recognition. How did this affect your leadership style and how you related to others? On reflection, how do you feel about this now?

- Reflect on your own leadership style in terms of the list of development tips above. How are you doing as a leader? Which of these do you feel you need to develop? As a start, select 2–3 of these development tips to focus on within the next couple of months.

A deeper dive

We are synthesising various aspects of these theories and the theoretical purists may find that we compromise many of the concepts. However, we believe that leveraging the interdependencies of theoretical constructs and concepts will bring some freshness of thinking. Our ultimate aim is the practical application of these insights in the workplace and to help leaders to understand and to expand their leadership approach.

We started our thinking journey at the most obvious place with Sigmund Freud and Carl Jung who position the ego as part of their theories of personality development (id, ego, super ego). Where the ego is the realistic part that mediates between the desires of the id and the super-ego.

We then moved on to relate the ego with the social construction-ist work of Berger and Luckmann in terms of how they relate the ego to the human capability of 'objectivation'. Objectivation is one of three aspects of human behaviour, the other two are externalisation and internalisation which are linked to intuitive and eco intelligence.

We also found meaningful insights for the development of the ego in the hemispheric structure of the brain based on the work of McGilchrist as mentioned in Chapter 2. Based on this work we suggest that AI may be an extension of the left-brain activity and plays and important role in the digital age.

The last source for defining the ego is based on the age-old traditions of the I Ching as discussed by Richard Rudd (2009)[6] in his monumental work on the Gene Keys. From Richard's work we gained many insights on the benevolent ego and its shadows and gifts. However, it is not only the concept of the ego intelligence that found grounding in this work, but also the other two intelligences, as we will discuss in the other chapters. We share four relevant aspects of his work:

- Richard draws inspiration from the Chinese Oracle, the I Ching, to develop 64 'Gene Keys'. The first two represents the male energy (Gene Key 1) and the second Gene Key, the female energy. These two are represented in all the other 62 Gene Keys, which represent various parts of the mosaic of our human consciousness. We relate ego intelligence with the first Gene Key, which evolves from its shadow of entropy (form-lessness, disorder, unavailability of energy), to bringing fresh-ness and beauty. The ego energy is the shaper, in that it brings energy and focus to formless situations and shapes it in one or other form of beauty.
- The second Gene Key, which relates to what we termed eco in-telligence, represents the female energy or principle as he calls it. It moves from its shadow of dislocation and fragmentation and becomes the binding force of all seemingly disparate cells, events, people and things. It brings re-orientation through rela-tionships and synchronicity that takes us to the ultimate sense of unity and oneness where 1+1=3.
- These two Gene Keys represents one of the fundamental exis-tential human paradoxes; our need for freedom and our need

for belonging, which drives our development journey as explained in Chapter 6.

- *In this masterpiece that is the Gene Keys, Richard also draws on insights from all religious orientations, quantum physics and other sources of knowledge to demonstrate how our consciousness evolves as individuals and humanity to express the radiance of our purpose.*

Notes

1 Haliday, R. (2016) How ego almost destroyed Steve Jobs' career, *Fortune Media IP Limited*, https://fortune.com/2016/06/14/ego-steve-jobs/

2 https://www.theverge.com/2019/5/10/18564625/elon-musk-vernon-unsworth-pedo-guy-tweets-defamation-lawsuit-trial-date-set

3 Berger, P. L. and Luckmann, T. (1966) The Social Construction of Reality, *Anchor Books and Doubleday*, Garden City, NY.

4 McGilchrist, I. (2009) The Master and Emissary, *Yale University Press*, New Haven, CT and London.

5 https://www.independent.co.uk/news/business/analysis-and-features/was-abn-the-worst-takeover-deal-ever-1451520.html

6 Rudd, R. (2009) Gene Keys: Unlocking the Higher Purpose Hidden in Your DNA, *Watkins Media Limited*, London.

Chapter 4

Intuitive intelligence: the Sensor

The intuitive mind is a sacred gift and the rational mind is a faithful servant. We have created a society that honours the servant and has forgotten the gift

Albert Einstein

Intuition... a black cat in a dark room?

For some people the importance of intuition is self-evident, indisputable – it is the source of breakthrough thinking, novelty and innovation. It is inexplicable but who cares? For others, intuition has no place in any sort of serious decision making – or business. Dreams, insights and eureka moments are fine for artists and composers but not in the world of management.

Intuition is somewhat like a black cat in a dark room, we can hear it meowing, but no one can see it! In this chapter we seek to explain how intuition works and why it is of critical importance to leaders in the twenty-first century.

Although we refer to some famous people that are known for using their intuition, Albert Einstein, Steve Jobs, Elon Musk or Richard Branson, there are many other intuitive leaders without a 'big name'. Everyday heroes who make a contribution in the day-to-day running of a business or a department, who apply their intuitive intelligence (mostly unconsciously) in meetings and when they take decisions. We hope that you will see this chapter as a prompt and an invitation to explore your own intuitive moments and be encouraged to practise honing this intelligence.

Intuitive intelligence: the Sensor

A medical doctor once made an emergency landing on a remote island. Stepping out of his small plane he noticed people curiously flocking around him. Some were touching him, some were listening, some smelling and others even licking him! He realised that none of them could see because their eyelids were sealed together.

He told them he was a surgeon and that, with a small operation, he could open their eyelids so that they could see. "What is seeing?" they asked. One person enquired, "Will I have more sensation when I touch something?" Another asked, "Will it refine my sense of smell?" The doctor replied that it would not but that seeing would allow them to perceive the world in a different way. No one was interested in his offer!

As he walked around somewhat bemused, he stumbled across a young woman sitting alone under a tree, looking miserable. He discovered that she was something of a misfit in the community but was willing to experiment with the operation. Two days later when he removed the dressings, the young woman was overwhelmed with excitement. She ran around shouting, "I can see, I can see!" The elders of the community tried to assess this new thing call 'seeing'. They didn't like it because it did not fit the conventions on the island. They feared it would destroy the way they lived and so they put her in prison.

In one interview a leader said, "I remember being told as a small boy that women possess a mysterious 'sixth sense'. I was therefore terrified of ever lying to my mother!" Since then I have learned that we *all* have this other sense of knowing.

The concept of intuitive leadership refers to 'a sense of knowing or perceiving without conscious rational reasoning'. It refers to our ability to 'sense within' a situation, but also to 'sense beyond' a situation into the bigger picture of the (yet) unknown space of unlimited possibilities. This often manifests as flashes of inspiration and insight.

The intuitive capability of humans is widely recognised. It is however still contentious in the realms of management and leadership. Decision making is expected to be fuelled by facts and figures, not fuzzy ideas and feelings.

Mindset – a world beyond boundaries

In Chapter 3 we argued that ego intelligence creates and works *within* boundaries and definitions, bringing identity to things and people as well as convergence and focus. We suggest that intuitive intelligence works *beyond* boundaries and linear focus, tuning or 'sensing' into the space of unlimited possibilities.

Intuitive intelligence needs space for freedom of thought and divergence in order to see original ideas, innovation and radical change.

Convergence can feel claustrophobic and suffocate intuition.

However, intuition is not only about new ideas, it is also about tuning into a situation. For example, a discussion or brainstorming session where one suddenly sees the real issue, and it is crystal clear. Also, when there is an elephant in the room, intuitive leaders are the elephant spotters! Whether they have the courage to name the elephant is another story. This depends on how well they are able to use their ego or eco intelligence, as discussed below. We call intuitive leaders the Sensors because they have their 'antennae' finely-tuned to pick up signals about underlying realities which are not always accessible through the five senses and logical reasoning.

Conceptual clarification

Before we discuss the gifts and capabilities of intuitively intelligent leaders, we wish to clarify what we believe to be;

- the difference between intuition and instinct
- how intuition relates to AI
- the physiology of intuition
- how intuition relates to the lesser known quantum realm.

We claim no particular expertise in the science of how intuition works: rather we wish to stimulate your curiosity – and invite you to sense what your intuition may be telling you.

Intuition and instinct

Do you see intuition and instinct as the same thing? Many scholars use the terms interchangeably. We believe there is a difference and make the following distinction:

Instincts are the (perhaps genetically in-born) drivers of action that enable organisms to respond to environmental conditions and stimuli without rational thinking. They are inherited, transferred from one generation to the next and reinforced by repetition. While animals have many instincts, humans have few.

Abraham Maslow (1954)[1] argued that humans no longer have many instincts in this genetic sense but rather that instincts have been overtaken by motivational drivers which are more related to cognitive maps than genetic maps. These cognitive maps form in our brains mostly through emotional associations linked to past experiences, and they inform our behaviour without rational thinking and decision making. These default patterns are often the result of personal experiences but are also part of our social and culturally transmitted behaviour. This conditioning is what Kahneman (2011)[2] refers to as System 1, fast thinking, which can be both helpful and unhelpful. Helpful when learning to drive a car but unhelpful when it forms into bad habits like unhealthy eating or overly emotional reactions.

Many leaders run their business 'instinctively'. Their past patterns serve them well when they need to take prompt decisions but some of these past experiences may not suit different or new contexts as they might be based on stereotypes and outdated ideas.

An elderly founder member of a Knowledge Management company told us he takes most decisions on 'gut feel', based on his 30 years of experience. However, the business context has changed radically, and the younger new leaders now need to be empowered to take decisions. They perceive his 'instincts' as opinionated and old fashioned. This causes tension between him and them.

We suggest that falling into instinctive patterns or automatic reactions based on past experiences is not the same as tapping into intuitive insights. In fact, our subconscious conditioning from the past can ensnare us in old patterns and reactions thereby preventing new thinking and intuition.

In contrast, intuitive capabilities reach beyond our experience and default programs into the unseen, non-rational and non-emotional realms sometimes referred to as the unconsciousness and the quantum reality.

We therefore argue that intuition is not necessarily based on past experiences. These realms manifest in our lives as flashes of insight or 'eureka' moments (suddenly understanding a previously incomprehensible problem), insights about difficult problems coming to us in a dream at night, synchronicities (coincidences with no causal relationship yet which seem to be meaningfully related), and déjà vu moments (feeling of familiarity with something).

In her TEDx talk 'The Power of Intuition', Katrine Kjaer[3] states that intuition is 'pure emotion'. We take a different view. We see intuition as something beyond reason and emotion. Emotions associate a positive or negative feeling with a past experience. These emotions can be misleading and cloud our decision making. Stereotypes are good examples of this. In contrast, we suggest that intuition is a deeper sense of knowing or sensing from a non-rational and non-emotional space. It often surprises us, and we are never prepared for it. But when it occurs, we should nurture it and prepare the mental and emotional environment for it to grow.

Intuition in a digital world

When leaders talk about their intuition or gut feel, the response from others is often sceptical. This explains why algorithms based on digital information are so popular. Smart machines can gather numerical data, store it and process it in an instant, much faster than humans can. It is said the IBM Watson computer is able to read more than 200 million pages of information in a few seconds. Watson won the Jeopardy general knowledge quiz against the best human players in the world. Smart machines beat the best chess players! It is clear that we have created something smarter than ourselves. So why would a leader explore any other sources of information, let alone their intuition?

Although digital computing has become quite sophisticated, the next level of computing, called quantum computing, is based on the principles of quantum physics and nonlinear thinking and will be infinitely more powerful – and the journey has only just started.

For now, let's look at digital information as it will be with us for the foreseeable future. Here is an example of digital information in its binary code:

a= 01100001 capital A= 01000001

b= 01100010 capital B= 01000010

ab= 01100001 01100010

One of the authors becomes…

01110011 01101000 01100001 01110010 01101111 01101110 = Sharon[4]

Even sounds and visual images can be stored in digital format then reproduced and transmitted at any time. This capability has revolutionised our world. Smart machines not only read and store information but can also create combinations of it. Following algorithms, computers can now write novels and produce music without instruments because the words and notes are all stored digitally.

As we have indicated earlier, digital information and algorithms are an extension of our left brain and ego intelligence.

Our intuitive intelligence provides access to the uniquely human way of perceiving and reproducing information beyond 'known' data, which may just give humans some competitive advantage over smart machines.

We have a wonderful opportunity to discover what it means to bring our humanity to a digital world!

The physiology of intuition

In Chapter 2 we referred to the work of Iain McGilchrist and the role of the right brain as the neurological basis for what we call intuitive intelligence. Intuition can be called the intelligence of the unconscious. Drawing on the right brain function, it picks up information such as electromagnetic and biochemical signals that have not yet entered the realm of language and rational thought. The right brain could be compared with a light bulb that illuminates the space around it and the left brain more like a laser beam that creates linear focus. We explore this argument further in the section on dreams and intuition.

Apart from the brain studies, McCraty and Zayas of the HeartMath Institute[5] show that the gut and the heart contain their own neural networks and have an inherent intelligence to enable non-rational and non-conscious ways of knowing. One of their research projects revealed how a person's heart rate variability responds to disturbing or peaceful photos shown on a computer screen a few seconds *before* the photo is shown to the person. This shows us how heart intelligence is able to tune into things outside of the body before our rational minds are able to process them[6].

Giving credence to intuitive intelligence allows leaders access to a whole other realm of information and insight. But it does require them to live more mindfully, and to cultivate the ability to *respond* (mindfully) rather than *react* (impulsively) to situations. By taking distance from situation and reflecting more often, leaders give themselves space and time to allow their intuition to work.

Intuition and dreaming

It is generally accepted that people dream every night in cycles of about 90 minutes, whether we subsequently remember the dream or not. McGilchrist (2009)[7] suggests that during REM (Rapid Eye Movement) sleep and dreaming, the right brain hemisphere experiences an increase in blood flow (particularly in the temporoparietal part of the brain) as well as increased electrical activity – when measured with an electroencephalogram (EEG). However, dreaming dynamics follow more comprehensive paths in the brain as some of the latest research shows.

Based on decades of studies by Solms (1999)[8] and Domhoff (2005[9] and 2019[10]) it is clear that a dream is not mediated through the analytical and conscious planning parts of the brain like the left brain and frontal lobes. The neural pathway of dreams follows a route through the emotionally charged and aspirational parts of the lower brain areas (like the dopamine release system) and ends in the more abstract, metaphorical part of the brain where visual images and symbols are formed. It bypasses the conscious reasoning and analytical or goal-oriented thinking parts of the brain. It is not driven by rational thinking but by feelings, sensations and aspirations. The images are uncritically accepted as real by the dreamer and gives them a sense of 'conviction and confidence' about the dream, or idea.

People with a strong intuitive sense sometimes talk passionately about how their dreams, whether night dreaming or daydreaming, have brought them insights about difficult problems and helped them process painful emotions.

It is likely that our intuitive intelligence follows a similar pathway as dreaming in the brain, giving us access to abstract thinking through images, metaphors and insights which are not always rational.

For us, intuition is not only about the neurological processing of information and impulses. It also involves tuning into triggers from outside, whether in our socio-emotional space or external stimuli in nature and even cosmic impulses. This takes us to the next section.

Intuition and multiple dimensional reality

Our efforts to understand intuitive intelligence would not be complete without reference to the thousands of years of human contemplation and experience of the non-material realm. Equally important are the latest scientific developments in quantum physics and the exploration of multidimensional realities. This has become quite topical in scientific circles since Einstein's discovery of the fourth dimension or 'space-time continuum'. It has been taken further by physicists like Michio Kaku (1994)[11] in his work on parallel universes and our multidimensional universe.

When Abraham Maslow talked about transcendence that comes after self-actualisation, he may have been referring to this state beyond time and space where we access other dimensions of our reality which have been beyond the grasp of our 'normal' sense of perception. Michio Kaku (2016), professor of quantum physics, describes how, as a child, he wondered about the fish swimming in a pond at a Japanese garden, "how they perceive their world, their universe?" These childhood dreams and questions laid the foundation for his search for worlds of multiple universes beyond time and space.

Our intuition somehow connects us with these other worlds and helps us pick up the signals we need to make sense of things in our material world.

If this topic is of interest, see the deep-dive section at the end of this chapter.

Taking intuition to a more practical level of application for leaders, we now explore the gifts, capabilities and shadows of intuitive intelligence.

The gifts and capabilities of intuitive intelligence

As in the ego intelligence chapter, we distinguish between head (thinking), heart (feeling and emotional) and hands (action) capabilities enabled by intuitive intelligence.

Head: the way intuitive intelligent leaders think

We realise that to link thinking with intuition may seem like a contradiction in terms, but for the sake of consistency we have included these as thinking orientations.

A sense of wholeness – seeing the bigger picture

As stated above, in contrast with ego intelligence which enables us to categorise and create boundaries, our intuition works *beyond* boundaries. Intuition's point of departure is the bigger picture and a sense of wholeness which expresses itself in every part of the whole. An example is that every cell in our body carries all 46 chromosomes that makes us *Homo sapiens*; or a seed from a fruit that contains all the elements of the tree and the fruit.

Holism is the opposite of reductionism (breaking phenomena into smaller parts). It argues that the whole is bigger than the sum of the parts. Intuitively intelligent leaders tend to start with the whole or the big picture, then work down deductively to the parts and the interdependencies between the parts. Seeing the bigger picture and working downwards to the elements instead of upwards enables these leaders to draw creative energy from a higher source or purpose. Just as each cell carries the DNA of the whole body, we believe that each project should carry the DNA of the bigger purpose of the organisation to enable a purpose-driven culture.

Continuing the storyline from the previous chapter, we refer to an interesting interview with George Blakenship[12] who worked with both Steve Jobs and Elon Musk. Blakenship explains that Elon Musk's purpose is not rooted in manufacturing Tesla motor cars. He has a vision of moving the planet from using fossil fuels to renewable energy. Tesla is only a part of that vision. When Steve Jobs developed the iPhone, his focus was not on the iPhone but on the App Store. For 3–4 years, Apple did not advertise the iPhone. The iPhone did not try to compete with Motorola and Nokia phones because Apple was busy with something bigger. Today Apple enables Google, Facebook and many other information platforms to function effectively.

Giles Hutchins (2014)[13] claims that an *illusion of separation* has been created by our left brain. It has driven egotistical efforts to break the world up into parts, creating boundaries that must be protected. Our intuitive intelligence restores the awareness of the fact that we are one with everything and everybody around us. A practical application of the importance of this sense of 'wholeness' can be found in the work of Jan Smuts, who became one of the founding fathers of the United Nations (UN) after World War 2[14]. His work on holism was key to the UN efforts to restore the sense of wholeness amongst nations. This sense of wholeness is a critical gift that enables us to contextualise and to see ourselves, our business and even our country as part of a bigger whole.

Intuition often manifests as a feeling. For example, this sense of wholeness might be a strong feeling about how things hang together or how to connect the dots in new ways. We cannot always define the 'big picture' but rather know it intuitively.

A leader described intuition as "the force of a magnet that draws everything into a coherent shape".

Hence our reference to the Implicate Order of David Bohm (2002)[15]. This leads to the capability of seeing patterns beyond the obvious.

Seeing patterns beyond the obvious

Intuitive intelligence enables us to see high level patterns in situations which can lead to resolving problems in ways which could not be discovered through detailed analysis. Strategy guru Gary Hamel (2008)[16] talks of the 'white spaces' which can sometimes be found between existing industries and sectors. These are spaces fertile for launching new products and services, creating new markets. Detailed analysis of current reality will not highlight them because as we said above, the intuitive mind works from an opposite holistic direction. Organisations that use rigid processes for developing strategy may miss these insights as the managers are engrossed in the rational processes of charts and checklists.

Intuition requires some distance taking and perspective; the ability to sense the sometimes still weak signals about what might be emerging.

Sony showed themselves to be astute at picking up signals when they saw the music and movie industries restructuring from the existing equipment suppliers and content providers into a more fluid and complex pattern.

Kim and Mauborgne (2004, 2015)[17] develop the same idea in their book Blue Ocean Strategy. They talk of creating an 'uncontested market space' (the Blue Ocean) rather than competing head on in existing markets with existing competitors (the Red Ocean).

Seeing new patterns is not only the ability to sense beyond, but also to sense *into* a situation.

Sensing into: seeing the elephant in the room

Emotionally intelligent leaders have the ability to tune into the emotions of others in meetings. They are able to work those emotions effectively. Intuitively intelligent people have the ability to tune into an underlying message or issue that wants to be surfaced. One leader told us how he always asks himself the question, 'What wants to be said in this situation right now?'

We mentioned the anecdotal elephant in the room in the introduction to this chapter. Many of us have had the experience of sitting in a meeting, listening to a conversation going around in circles as people argue. Sometimes this is because each individual has got hold of a different part of the elephant – the trunk, the tail or the legs – and they are clinging to their part of the 'truth'. We recall many of these instances, when someone just 'sees' the underlying issue clearly. Seeing the elephant in its entirety enables a leader to consolidate and integrate the issues in a bigger whole, often using metaphors or visual images. Combining intuitive intelligence with eco intelligence allows the leader to integrate the intuitive insights, then ego intelligence turns them into something tangible.

Intuitive intelligence needs a conducive emotional climate to function. When we feel under pressure, fearful and stressed intuitive intelligence does not work.

Frederick explains:

Years ago, I was in a top management meeting at our consulting firm. We as senior leaders needed to solve a problem. Everyone was trying to shine in front of the boss by offering solutions. These were shot down by the bullets of rationality and empirical evidence. It won't work, we tried it before, there is no budget... I sat quietly observing the process, enjoying my time searching for the underlying pattern, when the CEO suddenly called on me and abruptly brought my focus to the problem we were trying to solve. What do *you* suggest

Frederick? I pay you a lot of money to be creative, and we want you to come up with some creative ideas NOW! I shrank into the corner, finding myself unable to think creatively as instructed. I was worried that I may get fired if I didn't perform, now! My right brain would not function in this narrow space of rational and convergent thinking. I was stuttering as I tried to speak and explain that I needed some time to think. What I was looking for was an open and supportive space.

Sadler Smith (2010)[18] shares a survey of 500 entrepreneurs in the UK looking at the 'eureka' moments of entrepreneurs. The survey found that only 29% said they had their most creative thoughts in the workplace. A large proportion of 40% preferred silence and 27% said solitude was the best space for their moments of insight. The participants in the survey found other people's ideas restricted their own creativity.

It appears that the so-called brainstorming techniques do not necessarily release intuitive insights. My CEO would have done better to release the problem overnight and allow the senior leaders to go into their silent space and even allow their dreams to present some fresh insights.

It is this ability to connect the dots in a different way that brings innovation.

Innovative mindset

Intuitive leaders allow (and encourage) people to think creatively, to innovate, to move in leaps and bounds rather than be pedestrian. Innovation is easier in a small or start up business where the founder is often the leader and driven by their personal intuition. In a large organisation, smaller cells of experimentation are often necessary to allow intuitive intelligence to flourish and breakthrough thinking to drive innovation.

Intuitive intelligence needs freedom of expression and becomes claustrophobic in the bureaucracies of large organisations.

The French car manufacturer Renault invented the car category 'people carrier'. Ubiquitous today, it was revolutionary when the 'Espace' was launched in 1984. Infamously selling only nine vehicles in the first month of production it turned out to be one of Renault's most successful cars ever. Recognising the difficulty of innovating in a large formalised organisation where ego intelligence dominates decision making, Renault worked closely with a partner, Matra, to design and build the vehicle[19]. Learning from this success, the CEO Raymond Levy, created a process isolated from the main organisation (reporting directly to him personally) in order to create another new car category, the super mini, with launch of the Twingo in 1992. In a similar vein, Elon Musk was able to launch a luxury electric vehicle more quickly from a start-up Tesla than the established major luxury car manufacturers.

Intuitive leaders sometimes find customer needs to be constraining. The head of design in a fashion company described his frustration when listening to salespeople who think they know what the customer wants because they have their 'finger on the pulse' of the customer. In his opinion, customers don't know what they want. It is up to the designers to show them something that excites them. This difference of opinion often causes tension due to the fact that as 'money talks', the salespeople can often win the battle, leaving the design team despondent.

This is what Professor Noriaki Kano[20] means by 'delighters'. The designer wants to delight their customers with something that the customer themselves would not even have considered. As Steve Jobs said, if he would have asked his customers, he would never have developed the iPhone.

These intuitive innovators often provoke and challenge the status quo. However, they do not always seem to be very participative decision makers. They have strong convictions about what they believe and use their ego intelligence to mobilise people to achieve their intuitive dreams. Because of their strong convictions, they tend *not* to use their eco intelligence as much to co-create and collaborate. Intuitive leaders can become quite judgemental because they so strongly feel their intuition to be right, "I just know". As mentioned earlier, Steve Jobs was asked to leave the company he helped to create because working with him was too difficult.

Intuitive foresight

We believe that the intuitive playground is beyond time and space. Some intuitive leaders have strong feelings about the future, and many futurologists have well-developed intuitive intelligence. Bernard Shaw famously said, "Some people see things as they are and ask why. I dream things that never were and ask why not." This is the typical orientation of intuitively intelligent leaders. More importantly, they have the *courage* to step into the intellectually unknown – into the space of possibilities.

In 1953, Mark R Sullivan, President of The Pacific Telephone and Telegraph said in an address in San Francisco,

> In its final development the telephone will be carried by the individual, perhaps as we carry a watch today. It probably will require no dial or equivalent, and I think users will be able to see each other, if they want, as they talk. Who knows? It may actually translate from one language to another?[21]

Leaders using intuitive intelligence have a natural inclination towards the future.

They are energised by opportunities for developing new ideas and new possibilities. They are not constrained by today's empirical evidence or potential obstacles.

On May 5th 1961 John F. Kennedy said, "I believe that this nation should commit itself to achieving the goal, before this decade is out, of landing a man on the moon and returning him safely to the Earth."[22] This statement shows intuitive leadership at different levels. Kennedy intuitively knew that such a bold statement of ambition would engage and excite Americans at the time. He also believed from the data available to him that achieving it was a possibility, although by no means a certainty. And he intuited that it would reinforce his personal positioning as a future focused, young president. It was a risk but one that had been carefully thought through.

Heart: emotional capabilities

Solms (1999)[23] explains how intuition *does not originate as a feeling*. It draws on an energy that lies beyond emotion, but then it *manifests as a feeling* about something. Often as a sense of resonance or connectedness with something or someone.

Enhanced sense of connectedness

Most people tend to think of communication solely in terms of overt signals expressed through facial movements, voice qualities, gestures and body movements. However, evidence now supports the perspective that a subtle, yet influential electromagnetic or energetic communication system operates below our conscious level of awareness. Many people have always known this at an unconscious level. We 'feel' or 'sense' if someone is being genuine (or disingenuous), we trust or distrust a person for reasons we cannot fully explain. And we often recruit people on this basis. Have you sometimes found yourself thinking about someone and at that exact moment they call you or email you? This sense of connectivity is more than an emotion and requires more than emotional intelligence.

Being curious

Curiosity is more of a characteristic than a capability but it is fairly common in intuitive leaders. They are interested in general and evoke curiosity in others. This curiosity both triggers ego intelligence to do the analytical work as well as eco intelligence to engage and discuss the idea.

Intuitively intelligent people often read extensively, outside their professional fields, to explore what is going on in other industries and sectors. This provides stimulus, it triggers their thinking 'outside the box', "I wonder if we could...", or "I wonder if this is linked to that?"

Intuitively intelligent people, when confronted with an idea, want to know more about it and to explore its potential.

This is a very different reaction to someone whose instinct is to analyse why something is not a good idea, why it will not work.

Conversations with an intuitive leader can be exciting and motivating. This is partly because people are drawn to their insight and ideas and the passion they display, but also because of this natural curiosity. Because of this inbuilt curiosity they are often hopeful instead of fearful. In these times of the COVID-19 disruption, intuitively intelligent leaders are the ones sensing into a new kind of future, more curious than fearful about the outcome. They may sometimes even be regarded as insensitive to the pain and suffering in the world, of being emotionally out of tune.

Excitement and conviction: the eureka moment

Intuitive moments are unplanned: they come as a surprise like Archimedes in his bath. When an intuitive intelligent leader taps into some idea or 'eureka' moment, their excitement becomes contagious. They are convinced about what they believe without facts and figures. When we asked one such leader about the facts and evidence, he just replied 'I know that I know that I know!'

People admire these leaders in times of uncertainty and will follow them almost blindly because they caught the 'virus of their conviction'. Because of their strong convictions, intuitive leaders tend to challenge the status quo and can become disrupters of their industries like Henry Ford in the beginning of the twentieth century, and many others today.

Can intuition be wrong?

We believe that true intuition is seldom wrong. However, leaders often think they have an intuitive insight which is actually their instincts based on how they did things before, or it could be rooted in their unfulfilled ego needs. The best thing to do is to check one's intuition with others. For example, "I have this gut feel about that idea, could I test it with you?"

Behavioural capabilities (doing)

In the next section, on the downsides or shadows of intuition, we explain how to check insights from intuitive intelligence by using ego and/or eco intelligence.

Intuitive decision making

Richard Branson acknowledges in his autobiography that for him, gut feeling is a vital ingredient in his entrepreneurial judgment and business-venturing decisions. "I make up my mind within about 30 seconds of meeting them. I also make up my mind about a business proposal within 30 seconds and whether it excites me" (Sadler-Smith 2009)[24]

Think of some of the big decisions you have made in your life, like buying a house or deciding to marry your partner. How much of that decision was intuitive?

Many people would say, a lot! "I just knew that was the house or the person, even though I had done all the pros and cons that pointed me in a different direction!"

Cholle (2011)[25] suggests that modern society has developed a highly sophisticated relationship with the part of life that is logical but that we are much less eloquent when it comes to the part of life that is less logical. Intuition is not always regarded as an acceptable thinking mode for business decisions. Board members or senior managers will not easily justify their decisions as 'gut feel' or intuitive. Yet behind closed doors and often in retrospect, they will acknowledge the importance of their intuition when making decisions.

Intuition must play a leading role in complex decision making given that 80% of our brain is dedicated to non-conscious thought.

The benefits of such non-conscious thoughts are the activation of our deep experience, creativity, and problem-solving abilities. It seems likely that in the not-too-distant future scientific research will be able to explain more about how intuitive intelligence works by tracking patterns of neurological activity in the brain, heart and stomach. Currently it feels as though we are peering through the mist: we see shapes, distinguish patterns, build hypotheses and come to conclusions. However, although we see the evidence of this form of thinking 'after the event' in terms of the consequences of conclusions drawn and decisions made, we cannot yet clearly understand or articulate the process followed.

Experimenting and innovating

Many, perhaps most, successful entrepreneurs have displayed an approach to developing their businesses that required more than rational analysis. Often these entrepreneurs have been ridiculed before being recognised.

Intuition allows the mind to make connections that are not obvious at first sight.

James Dyson explains how he was inspired to revolutionise the world of vacuum cleaning when visiting a sawmill.

> The idea came to him after seeing a local sawmill which used a 30-foot-high conical centrifuge that would spin dust out of the air. The same technology, Dyson reckoned, could be shrunk down and built into a vacuum cleaner, omitting the need for a bag and ensuring the device wouldn't lose suction and become less useful over time[26].

He made over 5,000 prototypes of his cyclone, bag free vacuum cleaner before perfecting it. Initially he had no plans to set up a business himself but after several years of having his technology rejected by the major manufacturers, he finished up building his own production facilities. He told New York Magazine in November 2016, "I finally understood that if I wanted the technology out there, I'd have to do it myself." This is an illustration of how, because of its less than obvious logic, intuitive leadership can get ridiculed and presented as not 'sound'.

Leaders using their intuitive intelligence often require remarkable tenacity and persistence to drive their ideas forward to acceptance and action.

Experimenting is a key activity in bringing intuition to life, in making it tangible. Intuitive leaders invest in experiments as a way of testing new ideas quickly. They adopt a 'fail fast/learn quickly' attitude to innovation. Rather than doing extensive analysis to try and anticipate the probability of success or failure, or to decide which of a range of options may be the best one to choose, they are more likely to look for ways of getting things moving, quickly.

Experimentation is a practical outlet for intuitive ideas that cannot be rationally explained in order to achieve a significant development budget for an idea. 'Cheap and cheerful' gets things moving. One New York based magazine publisher used the expression, "show the dog the dogfood" when talking about new product development. By this she meant rather than spend several months planning to launch a new magazine based on market research, feedback on presentations of ideas to discussion groups, etc., take an idea, knock up 100 rough copies and put them in news kiosks around the city. Then see what the reaction is.

This may involve setting up a number of experiments or pilots to choose from when the evidence becomes clearer. James Dyson's 5,000+ prototypes bear witness to this.

The downside (shadows) of intuitive intelligence

Dreams and a lack of rigour

Intuitive leaders can be dreamers, always thinking about the next miracle! Their relentless pursuit of the next big idea may result in insufficient focus on more practical or pressing problems. Their constant focus on what 'might be' can seem unworldly and demotivating to some people. They appear to behave like a 'scatter gun': every comment triggering another thought or new idea. This can result in endless opportunities which never get turned into realities. Some people find this refreshing and energising but others who are more comfortable with clarity, structure and a degree of organisation find it disconcerting. They may feel threatened by it and challenge the leader (openly or behind their back) to 'get a grip' or 'get real'.

This may also show a lack of discipline or 'follow through'. Intuitive leaders may not complete things they find mundane or not important.

The focus on intuition can be used as an excuse for not bothering to do necessary rigorous analysis because it does not interest or excite them. It can lead to a failure to follow through on commitments and a failure to meet deadlines.

One of the biggest struggles intuitive leaders have is how to express or voice their intuition.

This is often because intuition is not based on rational arguments or business cases, and leaders fear sounding crazy or esoteric. So intuitive intelligence without a good dose of ego and eco intelligence is like an eagle without legs or a rock to make its nest. Therefore, we show how combining it with either ego or eco intelligence is important for its expression:

Intuitive + Ego: "I have been sitting in this meeting for an hour now and we are barking up the wrong tree, guys! ... Can't you see it?... We need to do x, y, z

Intuitive + Eco: "I have been sitting in this meeting for an hour now and have become aware of feeling increasingly uncomfortable about the direction we are taking. I am wondering if any of you feel the same way? Could we open this up for a deeper conversation? I have an idea to share.

Rigidity – having a bee in your bonnet

We mentioned the sense of conviction as a positive, but this strength may become the intuitively intelligent leader's weakness if they get so focused on their idea that they lose sight of reality. To mention Elon Musk again, he was so focused, even obsessed, with automation of his Tesla Plant that he ignored the advice of his advisors to better utilise human labour on his plants. His inflexibility cost him dearly but he was humble enough later to recognise and admit his mistake[27].

We know many people with good ideas but all they talk about is their idea, like having a 'bee in their bonnet'. They always try to fit others' ideas into theirs but find it difficult to let go of their idea and listen to others with an open mind. They also find it hard to give due attention and commitment to ideas that are not theirs. They may 'switch off' or become bored. We will return to this when we discuss eco intelligence in the next chapter.

Under the waterline

For an overview of how these gifts and shadows are driven by below the behavioural waterline factors such as beliefs, values and identity, please see the Dilts Logical Levels model in the Appendix.

Developing your intuitive intelligence

We believe that everybody has intuitive intelligence, although it appears to be stronger in some than others. You may think you are not very intuitive. Perhaps you are relying too much on your analytical left brain? A focus on developing your intuition may result surprising new insights. You dream but never remember your dreams, or do not pay attention to them? Intuition taps into the unconscious mind. In order for the unconscious mind to surface, we need to learn how to become *still* and to quiet our thoughts and emotions in order to become more *mindful* of all that is at play in any moment. Here are a few practices that you might find useful.

Spotting synchronicities

Synchronicities are small, unexpected prompts which if strung together may lead you in a certain direction. When looking for insight on a specific issue or problem try this: write your question on a small card and place it in your pocket and forget about it for the rest of the day or even the night. You may be surprised by the synchronistic prompts that appear, for example:

- a phone call from someone
- reading a newspaper article
- opening a book and noticing your eye is drawn to a specific paragraph
- insights arising during dreams or in the early morning

It is good idea to keep a journal or voice recorder next to your bed. Most importantly, learn to trust your intuition: we are usually tempted to attribute these things to 'mere coincidence'.

Mindfulness

Mindfulness can be defined as 'paying attention, on purpose, in the present moment, non-judgementally[28]. It requires us to be able to still the mind, and to develop a heightened sense of self and our environment.

Techniques include meditation, slowing down the incessant activity that occupies our every moment, taking distance and learning to laugh at yourself, keeping quiet when you would usually talk, being still and feeling/sensing into your body, then into the situation or the meeting – what do you notice? What is really going on? This gives the unconscious mind space to reflect and to connect thoughts and ideas in parallel with the conscious mind which normally dominates our thinking. It is helpful to practise mindfulness in day-to-day activities and meetings, as well as a regular meditation practice.

As your awareness of your intuition grows, you will start to observe your own and others' behaviour. Just observe, without judging or over-analysing. Do not allow your ego to react too quickly. When someone says or does something that upsets you, try just to observe the emotion of anger or frustration, but do not react. This is an important shift that will enable you to move from *reacting* (according to your habitual patterns) to *responding* (becoming 'response-able').

A variety of mindful meditation training programmes exist – both virtual and face-to-face. They create a foundation of skills for more mindful living, stress management and inner calm. A possible way to get started is to use the guided meditations on apps such as Headspace or Insight Timer.

Pay attention to your dreams

We mentioned how dreaming and intuition seem to follow a similar neurological path in the brain, mainly by bypassing the 'rational and motoric' parts of the brain. Many people find it useful to keep a dream journal or voice recorder, to record and reflect on their dreams. When we wake, we have a tiny moment of remembering and often do not know what to make of a dream, so we just cast it aside and move on. Carl Jung stressed the importance of taking a moment to reflect on your dreams.

Particularly to reflect on the *emotion* of the dream rather than the facts. It takes practice to interpret a dream. We found the article on 'holographic dreaming' by Dr Deon van Zyl[29] a useful guide in understanding dreams. He gives an explanation of how he dealt with the loss of his wife through a dream where dealing with the paradox of 'holding onto' and 'releasing' became evident in his dream[30].

Dream incubation 'sleeping on it'

If you have a nagging problem, try writing it down or reading something related to it before going to bed. Set a conscious intention to find a solution. Then release it and go to sleep. New and fresh insights may have come to you the following morning. Sometimes these insights are part of a dream experienced in the phase between sleep and wakefulness in the early morning, just before you are totally awake, and when your 'rational brain' is still asleep. A solution to a disturbing problem may become clear as you wake up and you then need to write it down quickly, before it fades away. This is what dream specialists call dream incubation.

Reduce your reliance on others for advice

When we are uncertain, we often turn to experts or friends for advice. While this has its place, it can inhibit your intuition and increase your dependency on others. When you learn to trust your intuition, you will feel more self-confident and motivated to pursue what you believe.

Frederick recalls an experience:

One of the most drastic decisions I ever took was to leave my academic career as a sociologist many years ago to become a financial advisor, selling insurance and investment policies. It was the worst time in my country's (South Africa) history as we were on the brink of civil war. My professors tried to convince me it was a bad decision. Every friend I knew told me I was mad to leave a secure career to take up a commission-only job at an insurance company. But deep inside I just knew I had to do it. I decided to stop talking to my friends and colleagues, to stop making financial calculations and just follow my intuition.

I remember feeling uncertain and very lonely, being the only breadwinner and having a family to care for. I cried the last day when I left the safety of the university building and walked into an unknown world. However, as I wiped away the tears, I felt challenged and curious. I knew very little about the insurance business and yet I felt a connection with this new career and I wanted to explore it. I took the leap of faith with hope in my heart and it turned out to be one of my best decisions. I brought fresh thinking to the investment and insurance world because I was not conditioned by the industry, so I was able to 'connect the dots differently'. I surprised myself in so many ways, especially when I got into the top 10 advisors out of 2,500 in my second year!

Spending time in nature

If, like many people, you find it difficult to meditate sitting in silence, an alternative could be walking in nature. Do not focus on a problem, but rather the nature around you; your footsteps touching the ground, your breathing, listening to the birdsong, picking up the aromas and feeling the temperature of the air on your skin. When your mind wanders (as it will), bring it back gently. Take time regularly to enjoy a moment of oneness with nature.

Set some healthy boundaries

People and life constantly demand your attention in a tyranny of the *urgent,* things that demand your immediate attention. This often prevents us from focusing on the *important* things (like self-reflection, self-rejuvenation and self-development) and limit our ability to tap into our intuitive mind for wisdom.

So set clear boundaries that will enable you to take time out to focus on activities that will help you to recharge and rejuvenate, and to remain intuitive. Remember…intuition cannot flourish when you are filled with stress or fear.

Do not confuse intuition with your fears or wishful thinking

It is important not to confuse intuition with long-standing fears. For example, a fear of flying or of spiders may have a strong emotional anchor rather than being related to intuition. These fears are often based on past experience – knowingly or not. Always try to check the authenticity of your intuition if you feel prompted to make a decision. Is this a moment of insight or just a deep-seated pattern playing itself out again? If, for example, you have no concerns about flying but on one specific occasion you feel it is not a good idea to fly, that may well be your intuition at work and you should carefully consider your options.

This chapter in a nutshell

The concept of intuitive leadership refers to 'a sense of knowing or perceiving without conscious rational reasoning'. It refers to our ability to 'sense within' a situation, but also to 'sense beyond' a situation into the bigger picture of the (yet) unknown space of unlimited possibilities. This often manifests as flashes of inspiration and insight.

The intuitive capability of humans is widely recognised. It is however still contentious in the realms of management and leadership. Decision making is expected to be fuelled by facts and figures, not fuzzy ideas and feelings.

We suggest that intuitive intelligence works *beyond* boundaries and linear focus, tuning or sensing into the space of unlimited possibilities. We highlight four points of clarification:

- There is a difference between intuition and instinct – we suggest that falling into instinctive patterns or automatic reactions based on past experiences is not the same as tapping into intuitive insights. In fact, our subconscious conditioning from the past can ensnare us in old patterns and reactions thereby preventing new thinking and intuition.
- We suggest that our intuitive intelligence provides access to the uniquely human way of perceiving and reproducing information beyond known data, which may just give humans some competitive advantage over smart machines.

- Intuition can be called the intelligence of the unconscious or non-conscious. Drawing on the right brain function, it picks up information such as electromagnetic and bio-chemical signals that have not yet entered the realm of language and rational thought.
- Our intuitive intelligence follows a similar pathway as dreaming in the brain, giving us access to abstract thinking through images, metaphors and insights which are not always rational, giving us access to the non-rational realm.

Intuition brings certain gifts to the leadership space – a sense of wholeness, seeing the bigger picture, sensing the connections between things and connecting the dots in new ways. Intuitive leaders are able to sense the 'elephant in the room', bring new and often innovative insights, often as a result of their ability to tune into the bigger whole.

Overused at the expense of ego and eco intelligence, intuitive leaders might be regarded as esoteric or fluffy. Many intuitive leaders struggle to voice their intuitive insights in the language of business cases, and this is where ego and eco intelligence come in handy, to ask others for input about their intuitive ideas and to assist in processing and shaping ideas towards implementation.

We are all intuitive and we can all develop our intuition further through practices such as spotting synchronicities, practising mindfulness, dream incubation, less reliance on others' opinions, setting healthy boundaries, and spending time in nature.

Reflection and application

- Think about an important decision you have taken intuitively. What enabled this decision? How did you experience this intuition? For example – flashes of insight, dreams, gut feelings?

- Have you experienced synchronicities in your life? For example – thinking about somebody then unexpectedly received a call or email from them?

- Have you been aware of your dreams? If not, would you like to explore noticing and learning from your dreams? How might you start doing this?

- Decide on 1–2 things you might like to implement on developing your intuition. Write them down and plan what you will do to develop them.

- How might you encourage your team to tap into their intuitive insights more?

A deeper dive

Hodgkinson et al states that "while there have been many conceptualizations on the nature of intuition, there is a growing body of research that suggests underlying non-conscious elements, such as implicit learning and knowledge and pattern recognition, which are involved in intuitive perception"[31].

Danah Zohar (2000)[32] *refers to SQ (spiritual intelligence) as the unifying, meaning-making capability of humans. She also talks of 'Quantum Leadership'*[33]*. She explains how our intuition never sleeps and often shares insights through our dreams, when we are asleep. When our conscious, rational mind is quiet, we are in the best position to receive the gifts of our intuition. Learning to access our deeper innate wisdom can help people discover who they really are and enable them to approach personal, social, and global affairs with increased wisdom, compassion, and positive innovation. We call this state of internal and external connectedness 'coherence'.*

Psychologist Abraham Maslow become known for his hierarchy of needs with 'self-actualisation' as the pinnacle of human fulfilment. However shortly before his death in 1970, he wrote about self-transcendence. This article was only published after his death and did not get the same attention as his earlier hierarchy of needs. One of the reasons cited is that psychologists do not normally have an appetite for the transcendent or spiritual dimension which is not easily measurable by the empirical sciences.

Transcendence refers to the very highest and most inclusive or holistic levels of human consciousness, behaving and relating to oneself, to significant others, to nature, and to the cosmos[34]. While self-actualisation refers to fulfilling your own potential, self-transcendence puts your own needs aside to serve something greater than yourself. In the process, self-transcendence may have been what Maslow called 'peak experiences', in which we transcend personal concerns.

In his classic work 'Wholeness and the Implicate Order',[35] David Bohm develops a theory of quantum physics which treats the totality of existence as an unbroken whole. Another gift of our intuition is to bring awareness of this wholeness or implicate order. It enables a realisation that everything and everybody is somehow connected, and that separation is an illusion. The implicate order is the deeper dimensions of our and the cosmic existence. It is the deeper 'enfolded' reality which becomes 'unfolded' in the explicate order of what we experience in our daily lives. This is why we refer to this space as a space of emergence, which our eco intelligence creates to allow our intuition the space to 'sense into' the deeper order. We believe that our intuition is our antennae or sensor into this reality and as David Bohm says, "The ability to perceive or think differently is more important than the knowledge gained."[36] The words of Immanuel Kant, "I had therefore to remove knowledge, in order to make room for belief" also ring true[37].

Earlier in this chapter we referred to the work of prof. Michio Kaku, who gives a different explanation when he refers to hyperspace and multiple realities. We certainly do not claim to be specialists in quantum physics but see an interesting metaphor in what has become known as the 'Einstein-Rosen' bridge (Kaku, 1994: pp. 224–226) or the 'wormhole' that connects two different universes. This idea has triggered the imagination of movie makers Christopher Nolan and others to make the movie 'Interstellar' (2014) which is about travel through the wormhole. Science fiction is claimed to be based on many of the theoretical insights of quantum physics.

The story by Lewis Carol, Alice in Wonderland, written more than 150 years ago also comes to mind. This humble tale has inspired countless films, stories, paintings and ballets. Even some neurologists have thought it sheds some light on the working of the brain as Alice slips in and out through the 'wormhole'[38].

Another author we found very informative in our search for a deeper understanding of intuition is Robert Lanza (2009).[39] In his ground-breaking work 'Biocentrism: How life and consciousness are keys to understanding the true nature of the universe,' he claims that the twenty-first century is the century where biologists will take the work of the physicist further. They will show that 'the 'old model' that sees the universe as a lifeless collection of particles bouncing against each other, obeying countless rules that were mysterious in their origins will be replaced by a new model that is based on a life force called 'consciousness'. Biocentrism revolves around the way a subjective experience, which we call consciousness, relates to a physical process' He challenged our entire education system as conditioning us with a mindset of a separate universe 'out there' into which we all individually arrived on a very temporal basis. Perhaps there is no 'object out there', perhaps we all share in the creative power of a universal consciousness expressing itself through us in every situation.

For us intuition is the way that consciousness relates to and connects us with our deeper sense of being, that does not belong to us individually, but is shared with all.

The last work we want to mention here is the work of Dr David Hawkins embedded in the science of kinesiology[40]. He takes the study of kinesiology further and developed it as an epistemology, or a source of knowing beyond rational analytics, that we want to call intuition.

He assessed muscle strength by testing the strength of a person's arm muscles when exposed to a positive or negative stimulus. A positive stimulus provokes a strong muscle response and a negative stimulus results in a weakening of muscle strength. The participant does not know what the stimulus is, but the body will respond positively or negatively. For instance, holding chocolates in a closed envelope will evoke a negative muscle response when asked if this is good for your health.

After thousands of tests over several years, he developed a scale of motivation or energy levels he calls levels of human consciousness. Starting with *shame with a score of 20, guilt, 30 up to the highest level of Enlightenment at 700–1,000.*

Danah Zohar and Ian Marshall (2004)[41] *developed their own scale of motivations based on the clinical work of Ian Marshall.*

Is this not where we as humans should focus our energy when faced with the disruptions of our time? Instead of only relying on data to save us from uncertainty, we could also be tuning into the unknown with curiosity and hope to find answers currently beyond the flight of our imagination!

Notes

1 Maslow, Abraham H. (1954) Instinct Theory Re-examined: Motivation and Personality, *Harper & Row*, New York.
2 Kahneman, D. (2011) Thinking Fast and Slow, *Farrar, Straus and Giroux*, New York.
3 Kjaer, K., https://www.youtube.com/watch?v=DJ71pKKDe1E
4 http://www.convertbinary.com/text-to-binary
5 McCraty, R. and Zayas, M., Volume 3, Number 2, March 2014, www.gahmj.com
6 https://www.heartmath.org/about-us/videos/the-hearts-intuitive-intelligence/
7 McGilchrist, I. (2009) The Master and His Emissary, *Yale University Press*, New Haven, CT.
8 Solms, M. (1999) https://psychoanalysis.org.uk/articles/the-interpretation-of-dreams-and-the-neurosciences-mark-solms
9 Domhoff, G. W. (2005) Dreaming, Vol 15(1), Mar, 2005. pp. 3–20.
10 Domhoff, G. W. (2019). The neurocognitive theory of dreams at age 20: An assessment and a comparison with four other theories of dreaming. *American Psychological Association: Dreaming* 29(4): 265–302.
11 https://cosmosmagazine.com/physics/michio-kaku-a-fish-out-of-water
12 https://www.businessinsider.com/elon-musk-on-starting-a-business-2017-11?r=US&IR=T
13 Hutchins, G. (2014) The Illusion of Separation, *Floris Books*, Edinburgh.
14 https://samilhistory.com/2017/04/28/jan-smuts-drafted-the-preamble-to-the-united-nations-charter/
15 Bohm, D. (2002) Wholeness and the Implicate Order, *Routledge*, New York and Abingdon.
16 Hamel, G. (2008) page 334, in Strategic Management, An Integrated Approach by Hill, W. L. and Jones, G., *Houghton Mifflin Company*, Boston, MA and New York.

17 Kim, W. C. and Mauborgne, R. (2015) Blue Ocean Strategy, *Harvard Business School Publishing*, Boston, MA.
18 Sadler-Smith, E. (2009) The Intuitive Mind: Profiting from the Power of Your Sixth Sense. *John Wiley & Sons*, London.
19 https://www.autoevolution.com/renault/espace/
20 https://www.mindtools.com/pages/article/newCT_97.htm
21 Sullivan, Mark R. (1953) *Tacoma News Tribune*, Tacoma, WA.
22 https://www.space.com/11772-president-kennedy-historic-speech-moon-space.html
23 Solms, M. (1999) https://psychoanalysis.org.uk/articles/the-interpretation-of-dreams-and-the-neurosciences-mark-solms
24 Sadler-Smith, E. (2009) The Intuitive Mind: Profiting from the Power of Your Sixth Sense, *John Wiley & Sons*, London.
25 Cholle, F. (2012) The Intuitive Compass, *Jossey-Bass*, San Francisco, CA.
26 http://nymag.com/vindicated/2016/11/james-dyson-on-5-126-vacuums-that-didnt-work-and-1-that-did.html
27 www.express.co.uk/news/science/1190979/elon-musk-tesla-artificial-intelligence-mistake-tragedy-spacex-open-ai-spt)
28 Reitz, M., Chaskalson, M., Olivier, S., and Waller, L. (2016) The Mindful Leader, *Ashridge Executive Education, Hult International Business School*, Berkhamsted.
29 Van Zyl, D. (1999) Dreams: Holographic Dreaming, *Cape Town Society for Psychoanalytic Psychotherapy*. Thoughts on ... 11(1) Summer 1999: 7–15. Further information on interpreting dreams is available at https://journeyintodreams.com/intuition/
30 https://journeyintodreams.com/intuition/
31 Hodgkinson, G. P., Langan-Fox, J., and Sadler-Smith, E. (2008) Intuition: A fundamental bridging construct in the behavioural sciences. *British Journal of Psychology* 99(1): 1–27.
32 Zohar, D. and Marshall, I. (2000) Spiritual Intelligence, *Bloomsbury Publishing*, London.
33 Zohar, D. (1990) The Quantum Self, *Quill/William Morrow*, New York.
34 Maslow, Abraham H. (1971) The Farther Reaches of Human Nature, *Penguin*, New York.
35 Bohm, D. (1980) Wholeness and the Intricate Order, *Routledge and Kogan*, Abingdon and New York.
36 https://www.brainyquote.com/quotes/david_bohm_130960
37 https://www.brainyquote.com/quotes/immanuel_kant_39
38 https://www.bbc.com/future/article/20150225-secrets-of-alice-in-wonderland
39 Lanza, R. and Berman, B. (2009) Biocentrism: How Life and Consciousness Are Keys to Understanding the True Nature of the *Universe', BenBella Books Inc.*, Dallas, TX.
40 Hawkins, D. R. (2002) Power vs. Force. The Hidden Determinants of Human Behaviour. *Hay House*, London.
41 Zohar, D. and Marshall, I. (2004) Spiritual Intelligence, *Bloomsbury Publishing*, London.

Chapter 5

Eco intelligence: the Integrator

If you want to go fast, go alone. If you want to go far, go together.

African proverb

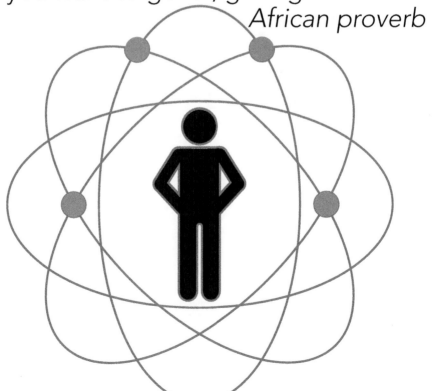

Leading in ecosystems

Although it has become fashionable to talk about organisations and even technological systems as ecosystems, few really understand what this means for leadership. The building blocks of eco leadership have become extremely topical as leaders search for new ways to be more collaborative, more agile and more human. Our dilemma in writing this chapter was the flood of interesting information and deciding what to include or not include. We present just a snapshot of the range of thinking about eco leadership and invite you to delve deeper when a topic catches your attention.

In the previous chapter we explored how leaders use intuitive intelligence to bring creativity, novelty and experimentation, seeing new horizons without imposing self-limiting constraints. In Chapter 3 we discussed how ego intelligent leaders create focus: defining an output or goal and mapping the route towards it. In this chapter we explore eco intelligence and how it is dominated by an existential driving force – connection: how leaders relate and integrate in order to bring together often diverse and disparate elements in a seemingly fragmented world.

While ego leadership is valued by those who need certainty and intuitive leadership is appreciated by those who enjoy the power of dreams, eco leadership is loved by the explorers. This is because of their interest in the journey – the *process* of enabling the organisation to thrive as a complex, living ecosystem.

As with the previous two chapters, we explore the mindset, gifts, capabilities and shadows of the eco intelligent leader. We end with some practical tips on how to develop your eco intelligence.

The figure below introduced in Chapter 2, shows how ideas and energy flow back and forth from ego to intuitive intelligence as they get refined and move through time towards realisation. Eco intelligence enables this flow. By integrating, synthesising and exploring, it manages the movement of energy from divergence (opening up spaces for intuitive insights and ideas) to convergence (allowing ego intelligence to shape and form them) which together bring the emergence of new ideas and innovation over time. We discuss this in more detail in this chapter when we look at the capabilities of eco leaders

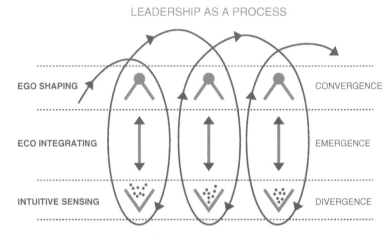

Figure 5.1 Spiral diagram depicting leadership as a process

The eco mindset: "I am because We are"

"I am because We are" is an African concept called Ubuntu. It literally means that a person is a person through other people. Eco leaders find their identity in relationship with the collective instead of within the individual. The 'I' expands as it identifies itself with a bigger whole or ecosystem. Naess (1995)[1] refers to this as the 'ecological self'. Martin Buber initially formalised this in his seminal book 'Ich und Du'[2] (I and Thou) in 1923, "A human being becomes whole not in virtue of a relation to himself [only] but rather in virtue of an authentic relation to another human being(s)". Eco intelligence is rooted in this expanded sense of identity.

An underlying driver in eco leadership is therefore the greater good and purpose of a bigger organisational ecosystem. An eco intelligent defining question for a leader might be, "do you feel a stronger resonance and identity with the entire organisational ecosystem (clients, stakeholders, the greater world) or with your personal needs for inclusion, recognition or status?" The answer is often *both* but they will be leaning in a particular direction. Another good question might be, "what does success look like for you?"

Understanding the organisation as a complex, living ecosystem

When leaders accept their organisations as complex, messy, living ecosystems they start to recognise the constantly changing dynamic as people from all levels adapt to prompts from each other and from their environment. This can be referred to as 'living in the space of emergence', where things are not always clearly defined up front, but emerge as you go along, calling on leaders to be tuned in and responsive.

The eco intelligent leader is curious to explore multiple perspectives and find mutually enriching standpoints.

As integrators, they often hold their own opinions lightly and are not the advocates or promoters of ideas, old or new. Rather, they play the role of the 'inquirer', bringing diverse opinions to the surface: not allowing them to be hidden away due to the fear of ridicule. Their focus is on the *process* of enquiry and exploration rather than the *content,* applying thinking tools such as matrix thinking, paradoxical or polarity thinking, divergence and convergence to facilitate the emergence of new ideas.

They do not seek that others should follow them personally but that they follow the common dream of the organisation and they desire that all staff should give expression to its purpose. They have a strong commitment to the growth of others and to building a sense of community. They encourage the different parts of the organisational ecosystem to self-organise and to freely express their unique ideas. They see their leadership role as ensuring that all the parts of the ecosystem are aligned towards a common purpose, and then to help conceptualise, integrate, share and communicate ideas so that all the parts can learn and grow. This is no easy feat. It requires a cultural context where people feel psychologically safe enough to express their diverse ideas, and where fear is replaced with curiosity.

Leveraging the value of diversity and inclusion

Eco intelligent leaders have an eye for diversity and practise the art of inclusion. They value diversity of thought and enjoy being challenged by people with different views. Eco intelligence is therefore essential when it comes to leveraging value from diversity and even opposition in the workplace.

As we see in so many reports of HR trends, diversity and inclusion remain one of the most important challenges in the workplace.

There is overwhelming evidence highlighting the business case for diverse teams. They are more agile, more innovative and even more financially successful than their peers.

Eco intelligent leaders see diversity as an opportunity rather than a problem. In fact, they will actively search for value in diversity.

They create the psychological safety for all the demographic categories of diversity like gender, race, sexual orientation, religious and other cultural orientation to participate fully and to feel appreciated for their contribution.

Unfortunately, the diversity and inclusion debate is sometimes seen in companies as only a socio-demographic issue. Although issues like equal pay and discrimination are important, we open the horizon to include stakeholder diversity and diversity of thought (cognitive diversity). Whereas ego intelligent leaders strive for a common identity in teams, eco leaders are more interested in a *growing or expanding* identity as they continuously include more diverse perspectives. They seek to involve all the key stakeholders in a value chain, including clients and even artificial intelligence, as an intrinsic part of the ecosystem: often blurring the boundaries between suppliers, customers and the organisation. This process obviously opens up a far richer understanding of opportunities for innovation within the bigger organisational ecosystem.

The work of Michael Porter (1985)[3] as far back as 1985 and many others who followed, brought attention to the importance of value chains in business. This approach brought a shift away from focusing solely on the shareholder perspective, to multiple stakeholder perspectives including customers, employees and suppliers. In the 2018 Deloitte Report on the 'Rise of the Social Enterprise'[4] it is mentioned as one of the major shifts in business in recent times. This finding supports the work of Hampden-Turner et al (2019)[5] who point out that leaders who proactively value and leverage the different perspectives or interdependencies between the various stakeholders in their organisations, with a strong focus on common purpose, will out-perform their peers ten times over a 15 year timeframe.

We take this argument further in Chapter 7 when we discuss cultural eco intelligence.

Who provides the energy?

One major difference between eco leadership and its counterparts, ego and intuitive leadership is the energy source. Is the leader 'driving' with their own energy or 'releasing' other peoples energy? Ego and intuitive leaders rely largely on their own strength and energy to shape the future and then to make things happen. Because eco leaders recognise the power of informal distributed networks, they work with the *energy of others* within the organisational ecosystem. They have the ability to sense into the natural, self-formed social networks and to help unlock their energy.

Instead of exercising control from the outside-in, eco leadership inspires a maturation of ideas, attitudes and skills from the inside-out, readying their teams for much higher levels of ownership and freedom to act.

They naturally prefer a more decentralised structure, where teams are empowered to make decisions and self-organise.

For this to work there needs to be a change in how teams work together (take on roles, make decisions, communicate, etc.) and what they expect from their leader. Decision making is devolved to lower levels, people are empowered so there is less need for formal hierarchy, reporting levels and seeking of approval for decisions. This enables them to respond quickly to emerging opportunities and take swift corrective action if something is going wrong. Some eco leaders even devolve activities such as recruitment of new members and performance review conversations to the teams themselves. New technology enables devolved decision-making and software systems provide access to information previously only available to managers. Getting this right leads to greater collaboration and organisational agility.

Eco leaders (when complemented by ego and intuitive intelligence) are key players in honing agile organisations that are responsive and dynamic.

One of the keys to unlock the energy from within the organisation is the subtle shift from 'getting buy-in' to 'creating ownership'.

Ownership versus buy-in

A local government asked a French consulting company to come up with a plan to rejuvenate the town. After months of hard work, the consultants presented a plan to the mayor and his team. Stakeholder buy-in was key to success and we were asked (at the last minute) to help achieve it. This plan would rejuvenate the town and create business and job opportunities. When the plan was delivered with all the bells and whistles of a good presentation, one of the community leaders got up to respond. He praised the efforts of the consulting company and the well-designed presentation. And the mayor smiled. But then the community leader said, 'Sir, don't call us to the dining room, call us to the kitchen!' (In other words, we expect to be part of the creation of this plan, not just a recipient of it).

He and his delegation left the meeting without committing to support the plan – and unfortunately that was the end of that initiative. We realised the wisdom of what the community leader had said: ownership (achieved by co-creating) was a better option than getting buy-in (with persuasive arguments once everything has been decided).

Many managers believe that 'telling and selling' their vision or ideas and getting buy-in is enough. We argue that it is not. Managers often think they can get people to buy-in by giving bonuses, recognition, and many live with the illusion that if people comply, they have 'bought in'. Even if people do buy-in, they will still blame management or HR when things go wrong. If, however, people feel they have ownership, they will take responsibility for success, look to overcome difficulties, solve problems and succeed against the odds.

Because eco intelligent leaders are keen to build connections and involve stakeholders in thinking and deciding with them, there is an automatic process of ownership.

They feel part of the organisation or team and have a deep commitment to its success. Hult Ashridge research into team engagement[6] found that in highly engaged teams, 'team members talked about feeling trusted and empowered by their managers and being given autonomy and flexibility to manage their own time, performance and results.' This approach very much reflects eco leadership intelligence at work.

In a reorganisation initiative at a European airport, the Field Operations team had been relocated to the outskirts of the main airport as a more autonomous unit. Instead of generating feelings of rejection and isolation, this change sparked a significant increase in employee engagement. The team felt that it had the focus and autonomy it needed. They were distanced from some of the negativity within the larger organisational culture.

In their words... "you'll see that in the scores of the employee engagement surveys, I would say over the last 48 months, there has been a significant improvement." Individually team members reported that they felt supported and free enough to try things out – and to make mistakes. They said of their leaders, "they allow us as individuals to practise what *we* think would be of benefit". So, there is never a case of, "We don't want you to do it that way, or that it's always been done that way, or this is the way it's done". "Dave (the team leader) will always give you the opportunity to put your plan forward, and even if you ran into difficulties, it wouldn't be a case of 'told you so', he'd invariably try and support you".

We observed Dave holding his team meeting. He would start by asking the team, "How are you all? Tell me what's been getting in your way or pissing you off in the last week?" Dave took it on himself, where possible, to remove obstacles and irritations to create a context conducive to performance (even the little things, e.g., changing their uniform trousers when they reported that it made them feel like bin men!). When we asked the team, "What would you say differentiates you as a team" the unanimous response was: "We are enabled by our leader and we trust each other as specialists".

Dave was not driving the processes, rather he guided the energy of the team, because they took ownership for the outcomes. Another way of unlocking the energy in the ecosystem of the organisation is to cultivate a culture of learning and knowledge sharing.

Eco intelligence requires knowledge sharing

To avoid chaos as hierarchy and controls are reduced, eco leaders often hold individuals and teams accountable for results (the *what*) while empowering them in terms of *how* they get there. With higher self-organisation, knowledge sharing to inform and inspire each other across regional or functional boundaries becomes an imperative. These leaders motivate their teams to realise the importance of sharing their knowledge and skills with others across the organisational boundaries.

As eco leaders have understood that an ecosystem flourishes if it is provided with encouragement and support, they see developing people as an opportunity and a responsibility. They feel rewarded by achieving success for and through others.

Eco leaders enjoy acting as coaches and mentors, as facilitators and enablers. They will often have a reputation for helping people get promoted and build their careers.

The groundbreaking work of Peter Senge (1990)[7] highlighted the importance of continuous learning. He quotes Arie De Gues from Royal Dutch Shell as saying that learning faster than one's competitors is perhaps one's greatest competitive advantage. And as the world becomes more interconnected, complex and dynamic, work must become more 'learningful'. This theme is still very much part of the vocabulary of eco intelligence.

Some organisations or teams have introduced learning or knowledge sharing days or sessions as a regular part of their calendar. The sharing of ideas and skills and cross-boundary teamwork is publicly recognised and some reported that it attracts talent to the organisation. A few teams we met rotate the responsibility to various team members to facilitate these learning days or sessions, offering something to stimulate thinking, thereby ensuring rich conversations. One of these teams had adapted a process they called 'each one teach one' where every team member committed to sharing knowledge or skills with at least one other each week.

In a 2017 article in the CNBC online magazine 'Make It'[8] Jonathan Ive, Chief Design Officer at Apple, talks about how Apple encourages communication and knowledge sharing. He is referring to the new Apple campus in Cupertino, California. Known as Apple Park, this giant ring-shaped building has been designed to be, "a building where so many people can connect and collaborate and walk and talk." The article goes on to explain how every detail has been carefully scrutinised, creating an end product that Apple hopes will foster even greater innovation. Responding to the challenge of fitting 12,000 employees into one building the article continues:

> ...it is a logistical hurdle that Apple believes will encourage collaboration between workers and between departments... workers will be more likely to build relationships with those outside of their team, share ideas with co-workers with different specialties and learn about opportunities to collaborate.

Another example is Google's g2g. Googler is the name used for staff members, and g2g is their learning network. Karen May, VP of People Development @Google says that when Googlers really need to figure something out, they ask each other. They turn to their colleagues for information, advice, and support instead of their boss.

At Google, 80% of all tracked trainings are run through an employee-to-employee or "g2g" network.

This volunteer teaching network of over 7,000 Google employees dedicates a portion of their time to helping their peers learn and grow. Googlers can participate in a variety of ways, such as teaching courses, providing 1:1 mentoring, and designing learning materials, and they come from every department of Google. Managers moved from a paradigm of giving permission for this learning initiative to giving recognition. That, together with technological enablement, energised the learning culture in Google.

Learning through face-to-face gatherings is now being challenged by COVID-19. It is wonderful to see the innovative new ways of connecting that are emerging. A new learning paradigm is appearing that is challenging the methods of traditional education institutions. Organisations are being called towards higher levels of flexibility.

Eco intelligence encourages organisational flexibility

A characteristic of organisational ecosystems is flexibility in structures, processes and policies. Eco leaders strive to know the unique interests and strengths of each person in their team and find ways to flex role descriptions around these strengths for the benefit of the person and the team.

In other words, a move from 'people to fit jobs' to a 'jobs to fit people' where possible.

Project-based work has become popular in eco orientated cultures, where individuals volunteer to step into a project role for a fixed period to reach a specific team objective, rather than follow a job description.

When Sharon joined the business school a few years ago, she had expected to be given a well-defined job description, as would be good corporate practice. However, when she asked her manager for a job description the manager suggested she should meet with her new colleagues to find out what they do and share what she has to offer. This included the sales, marketing and administrative staff as well as other members of faculty. By doing this, she could identify opportunities to add value. At the same time, they found what Sharon brought to be interesting and so the ecosystem adopted her. Today she is well established, having found her niche to live out her purpose in alignment with the purpose of the organisation.

From an employee perspective, this way of working requires commitment, maturity and ownership – but most importantly, a common purpose that rallies and holds team members together. The common purpose should be something that motivates them intrinsically because they find a sense of vocation or meaning through it: for example, creating a specific customer experience, educating a certain target population or changing mindsets about something.

A different lens on change and transformation

Change and transformation are urgent priorities for leaders in turbulent times. Ego leadership leans towards a more linear process where the leader defines the vision, the outcome and the steps to get there. They mobilise resources and people using the mechanisms of 'buy-in' as described above. But what happens when the outcome is not clearly definable? Clear 'end states' become quickly outdated in a complex and dynamic environment. It is known that more than 70% of large change projects fail due to poor planning, lack of proper training, and change fatigue offered as an explanation Forbes (2017)[9]. However, our experience is that it has a lot to do with the complex and fast changing environment. Change management consultants spend months working to determine the 'end state' and the 'blueprint' and how to get there. But when the change goes 'live' or is 'rolled out', the customer needs or the outside world has changed and the solution is no longer fit for purpose.

Eco intelligent leaders embrace non-linear change where transformation is a more emergent process involving the coming together of many smaller initiatives that emerge from teams at all levels, influenced by the informal leaders.

As definable initiatives emerge from the organisational ecosystem, eco intelligent leaders need to draw on their linear thinking and ego intelligence to ensure convergence and implementation. Agile project management frameworks like Scrum offer great processes to engage this balance between divergence and convergence as an iterative process.

Another reason for the failure of top down change programmes is that they often ignore or do not know how to deal with opposing standpoints. This brings us to one of the most important characteristics of eco intelligent leaders, the way that they deal with opposition.

Dealing with polarity and opposites

Eco intelligent leaders do not shy away from dealing with opposing views or paradox. They see these as opportunities for growth and they attempt to take the sting out of conflict. They are usually attuned to the underlying polarities and bring the opposing points of view to the surface.

One definition of eco intelligence includes the 'ability to deal with incompatibility'.

The acceptance of polarity is far from a recent phenomenon. Chinese philosophy uses the yin yang symbol to suggest that opposites may be part of the same thing or a bigger whole. In the Roman empire the Janus face looking in opposite directions illustrated the same point: that looking in opposite directions, rather than thinking 'either-or' may create new ideas. When we think 'either-or' we create blind spots and miss out on opportunities.

Eco intelligence can help to unlock the energy from opposing standpoints through adopting a 'both-and' mindset. This can be likened to two poles of a battery sparking when they come into contact with each other, until someone puts a lightbulb between the two opposing poles and gets the light to shine!

For example, Roche pharmaceuticals describe how they discovered their corporate agility in the interplay between *stability* and *flexibility* when they traded their 'either-or' thinking for 'both-and' thinking.

Many leaders tend to oversimplify complexity, reducing issues to: empowerment versus control, quality versus quantity, individuals versus teams, stability versus change or competition versus collaboration. While this kind of thinking has its advantages, it leaves us feeling that we have to make a choice. There is a risk that we either create artificial clarity or sub-optimise decision making – as exemplified by the expression, "any decision is better than no decision." Is it really?

Sometimes a decision not to decide is exactly what is required.

Eco intelligent leaders recognise the inevitability of polarities, many of which are paradoxical as part of life – including organisational life – and work with them constructively.

Roger Martin (2017)[10] refers to this capability as integrative thinking, which he refers to as 'the way that twenty-first century leaders think'. He quotes F. Scott Fitzgerald as saying:

"The test of a first-rate intelligence is the ability to hold two opposed ideas in mind at the same time and still retain the ability to function."

He gives examples of leaders like Isador Sharp from Four Seasons Hotels, A.G. Lafley from Procter & Gamble and Bob Young from Red Hat software; whose success lay in their ability to extract value from opposing views and form something new, instead of falling into the trap of either-or thinking.

Against this background of the mindset and views of eco intelligent leaders, we consider the gifts and capabilities.

The gifts and capabilities of eco intelligence

Concepts like collaboration, co-creation, inclusion, polarity management and generative dialogue are becoming well known in the new world of work. We have contemplated and researched these concepts for many years and have engaged in numerous interventions globally to apply these in organisations and communities. We have worked extensively with trade unions and management, facilitating this shift from an either-or to both-and mindset. In essence, this work has involved helping opposing parties to (literally) step into the others' world with an open mind, seeking to understand and engage in a more generative dialogue, resulting in often surprising initiatives from both sides. We have seen how the principles of eco intelligence are as applicable to large multinationals as they are to individuals and small teams.

We share some of our experiences under the capabilities of the eco intelligent leader. These are by no means exhaustive, but will hopefully provide a lens to reflect on your own leadership capabilities. We again use the framework of head (the way eco intelligent leaders think), heart (the way they deal with emotions) and hands (what they do).

Head: the way eco intelligent leaders think

The integrative capability of eco leaders is enabled by a distinctive way of thinking about issues. Here are a few of their thinking capabilities.

Divergent, convergent and emergent thinking

As explained by the spiral diagram in the beginning of this chapter, divergence, convergence and emergence are some of the thinking tools of eco intelligence.

By integrating, synthesising and exploring, they manage the movement of energy from divergence (opening up spaces for intuitive insights and other ideas) to convergence (allowing ego intelligence to shape and form them). Emergence (of new thinking and ideas) is the result of a good integration between divergent and convergent thinking.

The role of the eco leader is therefore not necessarily to provide new ideas but to facilitate a *process* where new ideas can emerge.

Their skills help to tease ideas out, paraphrase and consolidate for the sake of progress. As we have seen in Chapter 4, intuition needs a divergent space: an invitation to think out of the box. Eco intelligent leaders create that space because they are curious to hear and cultivate fresh, different ideas. It is at this stage that ego intelligence (theirs and others) needs to be drawn on, to shape new thinking and ideas and drive them towards implementation.

But how does eco intelligence deal with diverse ideas? Another capability of eco intelligent leader is matrix thinking.

Matrix thinking

This is the ability to look at a problem or opportunity from different perspectives with an open mind. Matrix thinking therefore underpins ecosystemic thinking and the notion of leveraging interdependencies. Geneticists have located this as a genetic capability which enables humans to evolve faster than other mammals in our evolutionary journey[11]. As opposed to linear thinkers, matrix thinkers look at a problem from different angles, invite different perspectives and ideas and ask, 'What if…?'

We are all acquainted with matrix structures in organisations. One common form is to position the operational departments on one axis with support functions like marketing and sales, finance, HR, IT etc. on the other. Or to have global product divisions on one axis and geographies (countries or regions) on the other. The underlying positive principle of the matrix (whatever the axes) is that it drives discussion, exploration of different views and subsequent agreement at the intersection points. This way of thinking brings a different understanding and application of the interdependencies in an organisation. However, people looking for clear reporting lines and a single boss, struggle with matrix structures due to the polarities and competing priorities they need to manage.

When facilitating a conversation between line management and HR we find it helpful to talk about the importance of focusing on people and tasks simultaneously. Ignoring either fails to recognise the inherent interdependency. Competence (skill and knowledge to complete the task) and engagement (the motivation to complete it as well as possible) are both essential to success.

Matrix thinking requires leaders to have the maturity and skills to hold challenging yet constructive conversations to leverage the value of the interdependencies between positions on the matrix.

When these different positions are opposing each other, things become a lot more challenging, and this is where the next capability is needed.

Integrative thinking and polarity management

As said above, the ability to deal with incompatibility is one of the key capabilities of eco intelligent leaders. Leaders who cannot see the underlying polarities when faced with challenges and problems miss out on opportunities for transformation and find themselves chasing their own tail. Eco intelligent leaders have eyes for and invite opposition or opposing arguments because they know how to deal with them. This involves both a thinking process – integrative thinking (Roger Martin) – as well as facilitated processes between stakeholders called polarity management (Barry Johnson). We share an example of an organisation we worked with as consultants.

It was a large industrial multi-national organisation. The business was almost paralysed due to the continuous conflict between management and the unions. We were called to help resolve the impasse. One of the branches of this multi-national organisation was not productive and head office decided to close the branch. It was not an easy decision, because the trade unions believed that, 'Injury to one is injury to all' and they threatened to call a strike in all the branches that would cause significant damage to the business.

We encouraged them to develop a joint vision, mission and values statement in a quest to bridge the gap between the parties, but it proved to be near impossible. Management said the mission of the business is to maximise profit for the shareholders. The trade unions concluded a more important mission was to create jobs and ensure job security during difficult economic times. Management argued that if people were not more productive, they would need to close the branch and jobs would be lost.

We had to find a different way to resolve this impasse or polarity and to apply our own eco intelligence! The challenge was how to 'integrate' the two opposing mindsets of management and unions. They were dependent on each other, yet miles apart in terms of their thinking and their actions.

Let's explore this idea of integrative thinking with a triangle and a circle. And let's apply it to this example of the trade unions as a circle and management as a triangle.

Figure 5.2

How would you bring these two shapes together?

Linear thinking would drive the ego leaders to hold strongly onto what they believe to be 'right', e.g., the union saying, "I believe in creating and keeping jobs (circle view) so I will persuade you, management (triangle) to fit into my circle, or the other way around.

Autocratic leaders tend to try to persuade or convince people to 'buy-in', or they may pull rank and use their institutional power to get the result they want. This was how things happened in that particular industry. We noticed a strong top down, command and control culture. On the other side, the unions used the threat of a strike to get management to 'fit-in' with their needs. Many organisations operate like this. It is a process of negotiation, threats and compromise, or rank pulling. In this 'fit in' mindset, there is always pressure to accommodate each other or to compromise. Sometimes the compromise is not satisfactory but the parties accept it 'for now'.

The following diagrams illustrate various options: For example, get the other to 'fit in with my way' (circle or triangle fitting in to each other), or to compromise by finding areas of common ground (overlapping circle or triangle).

Figure 5.3 Circle in triangle and triangle in circle

On the other hand, eco intelligent leaders attempt to integrate diverse ideas in a different way. They create opportunities for people with diverse ideas to understand the pros and cons of each, and then ask them to take distance and to explore new solutions that can integrate both. To extract value from opposing ideas and to create something new – a third thing that encapsulates the best of both. The circle and the triangle come together to create a cone. It is no longer a circle or a triangle, yet we can still recognise both in the cone.

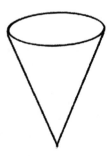

Figure 5.4 Cone (bringing circle and triangle together to create something new)

Often these moments of integrative thinking feel like a eureka moment as stakeholders see new possibilities that contain both-and. They have shifted their thinking to a third dimension.

This is what happened in the example we referred to above. We facilitated a process of generative dialogue between the two stakeholder groups, union and management. During our deliberations we realised that there were big gaps in understanding how the business works and why certain actions were necessary, especially on the side of the unions. We had various separate sessions with the stakeholder groupings to create common understanding and vocabulary about how the business works, the financial implications of not doing the work correctly as well as some technicalities of certain operations and the working conditions of the union members. This process took about two months before they were ready to enter into the next stage of the process which entailed us taking a smaller group of the union leaders, general managers and the engineering team off site for a few days and facilitating a process of 'generative dialogue and co-creating' the way forward. They openly shared information and together hammered out a new operations plan which kept the branch open. A £500,000 loss turned into £1 million profit after four months and no jobs were lost. They were all 'in the kitchen (vs in the dining room)' and had high ownership of the plan.

Heart: the way eco intelligent leaders deal with emotions

Building trust through understanding

Being able to create the cone by bringing the two shapes together is one thing but that does not help leaders deal with the emotions of their people. Leaders are constantly challenged with how to deal with the feelings of people who are feeling uncertain and fearful or who have lost trust in their team or in the organisation.

We highlight the importance of creating mutual understanding, and Covey's famous adage "seek first to understand before seeking to be understood". It is easy to trust people who agree with you because you can anticipate their behaviour. We have learned that if we cannot get people to agree, we need them to get to understand each other.

One of the leaders in our research made this observation:

> We had a dispute in our leadership team. I was shocked, because despite having all the facts on the table, they disagreed with me. I realised it was like trying to convince an atheist, using the facts of the Bible. They are not going to listen because they don't believe in the Bible. Nowadays I don't change a person's mind by trying to convince them to believe the way I believe, but rather try to put myself in their place and to see through their filters, and then make their filter coherent in the situation.

Understanding requires empathy and the ability to (even for a moment) step into the world of others. It does not mean agreeing, but rather to be prepared to see the situation through their eyes, and to imagine what they might be feeling.

Simple things like eating together, watching a sports game together or working together on projects creates an emotional space of being together outside the parameters of the workplace and also creates mutual understanding and trust.

Another way to create mutual understanding is through 'immersion'. This involves people spending time in other departments or countries to get a fuller understanding and appreciation of the unique circumstances and challenges facing colleagues or other stakeholders.

One of our experiences of facilitating such an immersion was in a large gold mine. Senior managers were encouraged to take the trip three kilometres underground into the heat and darkness of the mine shaft to remind themselves of the physical challenges that miners face drilling holes and cleaning up broken rock. On the other hand, union leaders ventured to see the smelting process and to see the real gold for the first time, the fruit of their labour!

Creating psychological safety

Psychological safety has become a major factor as organisations recognise the importance of engagement. It can be defined broadly as people feeling they will not be embarrassed or even sidelined for making a mistake, asking a question, challenging a viewpoint or offering a new idea. This happens when people feel understood and appreciated, and it cultivates trust.

Creating psychological safety is created quite differently by ego and eco intelligent leaders. As shared in Chapter 3, ego intelligent leaders recognise the need for belonging and provide some psychological safety by creating a tribal mindset of "you are safe with me".

Eco intelligent leadership, on the other hand, holds a paradox. It recognises that our *need for belonging* is complimented by our *need for freedom*, so it strives to make people feel accepted for their uniqueness and the way they challenge things in team.

This is an essential ingredient for the stimulation of new thinking, new learning and innovation.

It offers people moments in which they can openly discuss their fears, anger or anxieties about what is going on in the business. An important ingredient is the shift from *fear* to *curiosity* within the culture of the organisation.

Moving from fear to curiosity: finding diamonds in the dust of disruption

Fear is a useful emotion as it makes us aware of danger and the need to protect ourselves. A common fear or enemy can also be a strong unifying emotion as the ancient Sanskrit proverb says, 'My enemy's enemy is my friend'. However, in a culture where leaders use fear as a motivating force to get people to comply, it becomes a destructive power, destroying innovation and creativity.

Fear inhibits sharing who you are, your dreams and aspirations, your innovative ideas and the real contribution you can make to the organisation. Instead fear leads to self-protection.

Yet fear is prevalent in many organisations. It leads to people not challenging the status quo too much because of their fear of losing their job or being reprimanded. One of the biggest fears in the workplace is making mistakes – no one wants to have 'egg on one's face'. Fear spreads like a virus, infecting the entire organisational climate.

Initiative needs encouragement and nurturing, not punishment. Many leaders will think of at least three reasons why something will not work before finding one reason why it might work! For organisations to be innovative and agile, real encouragement is an imperative and cultivating curiosity is one of the most powerful things a leader can do. However, allowing people to voice their opinions, to experiment and make mistakes does not mean giving permission for people to be sloppy or careless.

It means recognising that if someone is going to take initiative or to innovate in their work, the first attempt may not be perfect.

Eco intelligent leadership aims to use mistakes as a springboard for further development and may lead to radical improvements in performance – 'Fail fast and learn quickly' is becoming a popular slogan in agile organisations.

Hands: 'allowing things to happen'

The art of facilitation

Eco leaders are better facilitators than judges. They shy away from the 'who or what is right and who or what is wrong' and are often not popular with those who want justice and clarity. They understand how to facilitate large co-crafting organisational processes. For these to succeed it is important that they do not hold too tightly to their own view of the 'right answer'. One leader said:

Over the years I have learned one thing for sure, ... not to hold onto my idea of the right answer. I have been blown away by the quality of decisions when I let go of my need to control everything.

This requires the ability to ask good questions instead of having answers.

Enquiry instead of advocacy: the art of the question

Both ego and intuitive leaders tend to promote their ideas, hence their preference for advocacy instead of enquiry. Eco leaders develop the ability to put their own opinions aside, or in 'brackets' as it were. They are curious and humble in their search for new ideas with an open (but not empty) mind. They ask more questions than they give answers.

In contrast, ego and intuitive leaders also enquire but with the purpose of understanding how they can help others to fit their paradigm of thinking. They listen in order to talk and influence others. Eco intelligent enquiry drills deeper than a fact-finding effort as it tries to uncover the underlying paradigm or narrative of others to understand their opinions and ideas. Because they are not there to promote a standpoint, they are able to listen and paraphrase the ideas of various stakeholders to create better understanding between them.

Open questions are invitations to share and respond, rather than covering up or reacting.

They provoke dialogue and cannot be answered with 'yes' or 'no'. For example 'in what ways might we...?, What do you like about..., What are your concerns...?' We often use a table of idea killers (e.g., yes, but we have tried that before...)' and idea growers (great idea, how might we do that...?) to help people get into the habit of practising the art of the question.

One of the most important tasks of an eco intelligent leader is to ensure that stakeholders have the required information and knowledge to participate in joint problem solving and joint decision-making. Unequal access to knowledge and skills is often one of the biggest barriers to overcome. Some organisations we met had created great knowledge management systems and interactive platforms to ensure this e.g., internal 'Wikipedia' with search engine, and 'Yammer Jam' sessions where questions are addressed and discussed.

Empowering others to act

There is a fundamental difference between sharing information (top down) and attempting to get *buy-in* via elaborate power points and charismatic influence versus creating true *ownership* through co-creation. Staff will only really take full ownership when some sort of response has been evoked from them and they perceive that the communication has been two-way, and that plans are the result of collaboration and co-creation.

Empowering implies releasing control and trusting teams to do things which may be different to how the leader would do it.

Leaders are often surprised by what teams come up with. Bâloise insurance company (see story at the end of this chapter) went through an extensive transformation process. The CEO agreed with his top team that it would be best that he withdraws from this process for three months as they felt his ideas would be too dominant and would not encourage others to step up. In our interview with him, he said that he had been 'pleasantly surprised'. He said that he would have done some of the things quite differently, whilst others he would never have thought of.

A different thought process and mindset are required to work in this way. The leaders have to let go of the need to know everything or be the problem solver. And sometimes to unlearn habits that are deeply engrained. Most executives are 'finely tuned problem solving machines' and are recognised and rewarded for this ability. The underlying assumption for an eco intelligent leader is that their role is to encourage and enable others to solve their own problems or rise to their own challenges. Asking good open questions like "in what ways might we...?" demonstrates the leader's confidence in others' abilities and shows a willingness to trust them. It also helps develop their autonomy whilst still holding their feet to the fire in terms of coming up with a solution. This is not an easy option or being a 'soft' leader but rather an option that requires an inner confidence and toughness.

Like the other intelligences, eco intelligence also has it downsides, if over used it loses its connection with the other two intelligences.

The downsides (shadows) of eco intelligence

Eco leadership is not a panacea. Nor is it a magical solution for leading in the twenty-first century. It is hard work, and on some occasions eco leadership is simply not appropriate, or there is risk of overusing it at the expense of the other styles. These are the moments when eco intelligence may slip into its shadows.

If the organisation is not ready

Trying to encourage a team to self-organise, if it is not mature enough, may be counter-productive.

When the mindset of employees is entrenched in dependency on a strong leader who shows the way and tells them what do, the shift towards eco leadership can be uncomfortable.

If employees enjoy having a boss who tells them what to do and takes responsibility for the achievement of goals, they may perceive a move towards participation and joint decision making as a capitulation of management responsibility. As one of the team members told us after the boss tried to be eco intelligent and asked them to define their own jobs: 'He gets paid to develop our job profiles and targets, why should we do it?'

On a more personal level, some staff may be strongly rooted in their own ego needs for security (wanting clear job descriptions, secure jobs for life, stable work environment), or a need for belonging (wanting to feel their team is like a caring family with the team leader as protective mother or father figure). Or they may need differentiation and status (wanting to stand out as 'the special ones' above others). These relationships can emulate the dynamics of a parent to child between leader and team rather than the adult to adult dynamic required for eco leadership to be successful.

Apart from the employees not being ready, sometimes leaders are not ready to release control. In some organisations where we co-developed structures and processes for joint decision making, some managers continued their micro-management and command and control actions, because this had become their comfort zone over many years. They were not emotionally ready to change.

We cannot try to give wings to a caterpillar, flying is the result of an internal transformation process, which we discuss in Chapter 6.

Inertia... incessant talk shops with little action

Because eco leaders value the inclusion of all stakeholders, they may be inclined to open up too many spaces or ideas for conversation and collaboration.

This can result in continuous divergence and endless discussion of a topic. The inability to converge or close to a point where a decision can be taken, leads to inaction.

Some of the leaders in the research said that in their organisation the pendulum had swung too far towards eco leadership at the expense of decision making, speed and efficiency (ego leadership). One CEO said:

> I am the integrator, so the criticism I get is, 'why is he so slow?' I am often perceived as unclear in my position, of not putting my view forward and taking a stand. I hold too many bi-lateral conversations to get all the individuals on board first. This is time-consuming and I end up changing with each conversation, creating much confusion in the leadership team.

Conflict avoidance

Eco leaders value mutual respect, humility and inclusion. This sometimes leads to a reluctance or even discomfort with confronting issues and dealing with conflict. One of the leaders referred to their culture as having a "high human factor where everyone is always nice to each other". The flipside to this is a reluctance and even inability to deal with conflict and make unpopular decisions. Eco leaders may become so sensitive to the needs of people that they lose sight of the business needs and goals and refrain from giving clear direction.

Eco leaders hold their opinions lightly which is good when one wants to open up discussion and co-creation, but when clear decision making is required, the eco leader needs to switch on their ego intelligence and bring direction and clarity.

Under the waterline

For an overview of how these gifts and shadows are driven by below the behavioural waterline factors such as values, beliefs and sense of identity, please see the Dilts Logical Levels model in the Appendix.

Developing your eco intelligence

The table below is a summary of suggestions shared by participants in workshops and discussions during our research:

Head-thinking	Heart-feeling	Hands-doing
Divergent, convergent and emergent thinking: • Ensure an understanding of the underlying purpose • Allow for new ways of expression of purpose • Look for connections between ideas: connect the dots	Building trust through understanding: • First seek to understand, then to be understood Creating psychological safety: • Create an organisational culture of high care and high trust. • Ensure informal/ social engagement between people • Encourage and don't punish initiative & ideas • Encourage challenge & different opinions to surface	Practising the art of facilitation: • Create opportunities for regular thinking together • Take distance – Learn to let go and to trust the process

Head-thinking	Heart-feeling	Hands-doing
Matrix Thinking: • Encourage different perspectives on ideas and opportunities • Engage with other points of view, explore differences of opinion	Moving from fear to curiosity: • Create a 'feedback fit 'culture where feedback is regularly sought and given • Ask what we can learn from what is happening • Find diamonds in the dust of disruption and disappointment	Enquiry instead of advocacy - the art of the question: • Posing questions rather than giving answers • Practise active listening, with an open (not an empty) mind & open heart
Practising integrative thinking and polarity management: • Accept polarities and paradoxes as normal • Drill down beyond the presenting problem and search for the underlying paradox • Look for both-and rather than either-or solutions • Extract value from opposite ideas	Practising empathy and immersion: • Express appreciation for contributions • Believe in the inherent good in others and their standpoints • Balance self-interest with generosity and concern for others • Immerse yourself in the work context of others	Empowering others to act: • Share the leadership space with others. • Encourage self-managing teams • Be transparent and share information to enable joint decision making • Reduce hierarchies to create networks of teams with linking people. • Point out and leverage (create value from) interdependencies between teams

This chapter in a nutshell

Eco intelligence is the essential ingredient that brings leadership agility. It can be described as a dynamic process of integration. This process is embedded in an underlying ecosystemic mindset and applied through various capabilities we discussed under the subheadings of Head (thinking), Heart (feeling) and Hands (doing). Eco leaders see the organisation as a complex, living system, where diversity flourishes because it has learnt the art of inclusion and integration.

Eco intelligent leaders do not work with their own energy to drive their ideas into fruition but with the energy of others as they strive to leverage the whole ecosystem. They promote a sense of ownership instead of attempting to get buy-in. They achieve this ownership by focusing on asking good questions and facilitating processes that stimulate ownership and co-creation.

They cultivate a learning culture by striving to unlock the potential of people through continuous knowledge sharing and learning. Learning here is not only the transfer of knowledge, but also the peer to peer sharing of experience and reflections on what is working well and not in the organisation.

Eco intelligence encourages flexibility in structures, processes and policies to enable the organisation to self-organise especially regarding the way that people define their work.

Rather than viewing change and transformation as a linear process, it sees transformation as an emergent process where the outcomes are not always definable. It has the wisdom to hold lightly onto a clearly defined outcome, but also to let go of it and allow something new to emerge. Developing a keen eye for the underlying paradoxes as part of human and organisational life, and recognising the power of reconciling opposites instead of eliminating them, makes eco intelligence a vital ingredient of thriving organisations.

The downsides of eco intelligence occur when the organisation or a team is not ready because of their need for strong top down direction or security. Too much eco with too little ego intelligence can lead to incessant talk shops as eco leaders continue to open up divergent spaces for dialogue, which are time consuming and sometimes lack decision making and focus. Because eco leaders embrace mutual respect and want to accommodate everyone, it may lead to avoiding conflict and taking unpopular decisions.

Reflection and application

- Can you identify eco leaders in your organisation? What skills and capabilities do see in them?

- How are you doing as an eco intelligent leader?

- How do you feel about involving others more in thinking together (co-crafting) and joint decision making?

- How might you release control on 'how' your teams operate?

- What are the risks to you of taking a more eco intelligent approach?

- What behaviours are you encouraging, recognising and rewarding in your teams?

- What eco skills or capabilities do you need to improve?

- How can you avoid the shadow side of overdoing eco intelligence?

A deeper dive

Eco Intelligence and Spiritual Intelligence

Danah Zohar and Ian Marshall bring together insights from neuro-science, philosophy and quantum physics. They define IQ as the brain's 'serial thinking' capability, which enables linear, logical and cause-effect reasoning. It is finite, works within boundaries and is useful when we need to scan new horizons and the unexpected: this relates to what we called 'ego intelligence'. They go further to relate EQ, or Emotional Intelligence to the associative thinking ability of the brain. These neural networks draw links (associations) between emotions, bodily experiences and concepts. This is the basis of classical conditioning as in the experiments of the Russian scientist Pavlov with dogs. For instance, one learns certain skills like driving a car through repetition and association and cannot necessarily explain the rules, you just do it. These associative networks can lead to what we call 'stuckness' which we have discussed in the 'downside of the ego' section and in our discussion of human instincts in Chapter 4 on intuitive intelligence.

They introduce Spiritual Intelligence as that special capability of the human brain, when neurons oscillate around 40 Hz, to contextualise and give meaning, and most importantly, it gives us the ability for what they call 'unitive thinking' or seeing the bigger picture. They base their argument on the work of neurologist Wolf Singer and Charles Grey (2006)[12] from Frankfurt. SQ gives us our ability of self-awareness and transcendence and gives us our transformative ability or our ability to rewire our brain. Danah Zohar (1994)[13] applied these concepts in the business world in her work 'Rewiring the Corporate Brain'. Zohar (2016)[14] takes these ideas further in the 'Quantum Leader: using new science to rethink how we structure and lead organisations.'

Our concepts of intuitive and eco intelligence draw on Zohar's concepts of Spiritual Intelligence and Quantum Leadership.

Eco leadership – the fourth discourse

We build on the work of Simon Western who describes eco leadership as the fourth discourse in leadership for the twenty-first century after the Controller (1900s Scientific Management), the Therapist (1960s Humans Relations – EQ) and the Messiah (1980s – Transformational culture control). He suggests that the prefix 'eco' signifies how progressive leaders conceptualise organisations as ecosystems and networks rather than closed systems. He clarifies that an ecosystem requires nurturing, not control. "Eco leadership recognises that within an organisation there are interdependent parts which make up a whole, this goes for all stakeholder relationships, and in ever widening circles that eventually reach the air that we breathe. It is about connectivity, interdependence and sustainability underpinned by an ethical and socially responsible stance"[15].

Ego system awareness vs. ego system reality

Our initial inspiration for coining 'ego and eco intelligence' comes from the influential work of Otto Scharmer and Katrin Kaufer (2013.)[16] They argue that there is a strong link between thought and social reality. They point to the disconnect between the way the ego thinks (ego awareness) and the (eco) reality of the world out there. It works like an ecosystem; economic, political, socio-cultural and environmental systems are intertwined, uncertain and highly complex. This disconnect of approaching a complex eco-systemic reality with an ego mindset is one of the major problems facing leaders today.

They refer to the problems of the EU in this regard and argue that many of its problems are the result of this disconnect. For example, the narrow ego awareness of each country (national interests focus) prevents leaders from really harvesting the benefits that come from creating value from a more integrated common good, or in our terms, applying eco intelligence.

Theory U, Scharmer (2009)[17] presents a good 'eco intelligent' process where leaders can overcome their blind spots based on past experience and open the horizon for something new to emerge. Some of the qualities that are critical to what we call eco intelligence are embedded in the three concepts he uses: an open mind, an open heart and an open will. This process is widely used to facilitate generative dialogue in teams and we highly recommend it for those who want to apply their eco intelligence in complex environments.

Notes

1 Naess, A. (1995) Self-realization. An ecological approach to being in the world. In G. Sessions (ed), Deep Ecology for the 21st Century. Readings on the Philosophy and Practice of the New Environmentalism. *Shambala*, Boston, MA, pp. 225–239.
2 Buber, M. (1923) Ich und Du, *Insel-Verlag*, Leipzig.
3 Porter, M. (1985) Competitive Advantage: Creating and Sustaining Superior Performance, *Simon and Schuster*, New York.
4 https://www2.deloitte.com/content/dam/Deloitte/at/Documents/human-capital/at-deloitte-insights-the-rise-of-the-social-enterprise.pdf
5 Hampden-Turner, C., O'Riordan, L., and Trompenaars, F., (2019) Capitalism in Crisis, *Filament Publishing*, Croydon.
6 Armstrong, A., Olivier, S., and Wilkinson, S. (2018) Shades of Grey: An Exploratory Study of Engagement in Work Teams, *Hult Ashridge Executive Education*, Berkhamsted.
7 Senge, P. (1990) The Fifth Discipline: The Art and Practice of the Learning Organization. *Doubleday Dell Publishing Group Inc.*, New York.

8 https://www.cnbc.com/2017/09/13/the-science-and-design-behind-apples-innovation-obsessed-new-workspace.html

9 https://www.forbes.com/sites/brentgleeson/2017/07/25/1-reason-why-most-change-management-efforts-fail/#13b91a37546b

10 Martin, R. (2017) Creating Great Choices: A Leader's Guide to Integrative Thinking, *Harvard Business Review Press*, Boston, MA.

11 Uhlhaas, P. J. and Singer, W. (2006) Neural synchrony in brain disorders: Relevance for cognitive dysfunctions and pathophysiology. *Neuron* 52: 155–168.

12 Zohar, D. (1994) Rewiring the Corporate Brain, *Berrett-Koehler*, Oakland, CA.

13 Zohar, D. (2016) The Quantum Leader, *Prometheus Books*, New York.

14 Western, S. (2008) Leadership: A Critical Text, *Sage Publishing*, London.

15 Scharmer, O. and Kaufer, K., (2013) Leading from the Emerging Future. *Berrett-Koehler Publisher*, San Francisco, CA.

16 Scharmer, C. O. (2009) Theory U, Leading from the Future as It Emerges. *Berrett-Koehler Publishers*, San Francisco, CA.

Chapter 6

The personal development journey

The journey is the destination

Not for the faint hearted

A journey of personal development is a lifetime's work involving courage and determination. As Stephen Covey (1989)[1] says, "almost every significant breakthrough is the result of the courage to break with the traditional ways of working". We suggest that perhaps the journey is the destination. It is learning what to hold onto and having the courage to let go.

We are all, as human beings, curious: we seek to explore and to understand, we reflect on things. This the nature of learning. We (the authors) believe that learning and leading are synonymous: the person who has lost their interest in learning will not be a good leader. As we learn about ourselves and understand our own experiences better, we become more self-aware and more able to act thoughtfully – some might say 'choicefully' – allowing us to bring the best of ourselves to our work as leaders and our lives overall.

Many people: philosophers ancient and modern, psychologists, scientists, theologists and more, have tried to explain how human consciousness develops. Put simply – how people learn, how they grow, how they make sense/meaning, and what they become aware of at various stages of their journey. There are a number of different frameworks to explain it.

In this chapter we explore development as a reflexive journey. The essence of the reflexive development journey is always the same: greater self-awareness and self-understanding develops through reflecting on powerful experiences we live through and allowing ourselves to be changed and expanded by these experiences. We call these 'crucible moments' where something happens with intensity and heat, as in a crucible. These experiences provide opportunities for learning and growth through reflection and exploration or they can be ignored, 'buried' perhaps, as too uncomfortable. We start this chapter with a personal example of a crucible moment.

Frederick's story

The early years of Frederick's working life were spent as a sociologist at the University of South Africa in Pretoria in the 1970s. Painfully aware of the fragmentation of South African society, he and a number of colleagues decided that the best way to try and restore unity and prosperity to their country was to use an approach known as 'generative dialogue'. This entailed holding open, constructive conversations, trying to bridge disagreements step-by-step, showing tolerance of different views, building mutual understanding, then slowly allowing a new reality to emerge.

This approach was not popular with the extremists who ruled on either side of the racial divide. The white regime, driven by fear, believed that more stringent controls would save the day while the black comrades, fuelled by anger and a need for liberation, believed that one day they, the under-privileged, would take over the majority rule of the country. In this whirlpool of anxiety, frustration, anger and fear, the 'apartheid' system was starting to shake.

In the 1980s Frederick left academia to become a management consultant. He had a passion to help bring reconciliation to South Africa through generative dialogue. His first consulting assignment was to help bring law and order back into some black schools and Colleges of Education which were in chaos. Thus, four years before Nelson Mandela was set free, Frederick found himself in the eye of the storm of a collapsing apartheid system, trying to bridge the gap between angry students who were part of the struggle for liberation and an educational establishment desperately trying to keep the lid on a boiling pot. It was clear that there were two entrenched systems in conflict. On the one hand, the students who had never been involved in the management of schools but were driven by their mantra of 'liberation before education' and on the other, the Department of Education leadership who wanted to use their command and control approach to maintain the education system that had become the symbol of oppression.

He vividly recalls an episode at a College of Education in a black township on the outskirts of Johannesburg. The Student Representative Council had called the Rector out as a racist and issued threats to him and some other lecturers. Frederick and some colleagues were called in as consultants by the Department of Education to help re-establish order. The Department believed that the return of the Rector was essential: ousting the Rector was certainly not an option.

Trust was in short supply. The best Frederick and his colleagues could hope for was that the stakeholders would at least listen to each other: to understand each other without necessarily agreeing. They facilitated a number of sessions to try to create a mutual understanding. After a few weeks, a tense agreement was reached. The Department (represented by the Regional Director) agreed to meet publicly with the students to respond to their demands in an attempt to restore the credibility of the Rector as head of the College, and to enable the teachers to get back to work. As consultants, Frederick and his colleagues carefully crafted a speech which they hoped would persuade the students to allow the Rector to return to the College. The plan was for the Regional Director to deliver the speech, supported by the Vice Rector, with Frederick present as a facilitator. Frederick takes up the tale...

The day arrived when we had to address the students in an open forum. We walked on stage, three WAMs (White Afrikaner Men) to face a hall of 600 raucous students chanting and mocking us with an Afrikaans song, 'Oh, the donkey is a wonderful thing, he stands in the passage and tries to scare me, oh the donkey is a wonderful thing'. The Regional Director immediately picked up on the unspoken expectations in the room and the dangerous tension lying just below the surface. He glanced at me as we walked to the stage in the hall and said: 'I'm not going to deliver this speech Frederick: you can do it.' This came as a shock to me as I had not signed up or prepared for it, but I realised I had no choice. We walked onto the stage and there I stood, centre-stage, with 600 chanting students glaring furiously at us.

I knew intuitively from my experience over the previous few weeks that advocating the return of the Rector at this point would ignite the emotional dynamite in the room. Nonetheless, I started with the pre-planned speech, filled with statistics, inspirational quotes and clear direction. I did not get very far as the students mocked me and shouted me down. A loud voice roared from the back of the hall, 'Don't you see comrades, he is just another white man trying to defend the apartheid system!' At that moment the mood in the hall changed from mocking to palpable anger and I knew from experience how this could end: I feared for our lives.

My primitive fight or flight brain screamed at me to run away from the anger and frustration crashing down on me and the other two men on the stage. Previous warnings of such danger flashed through my mind. I remembered my history teacher telling me about the threats we would face as an Afrikaner nation – losing our identity, our land, our country and our lives – and here we were!

It was in the middle of this mayhem that something strange but wonderful happened within me. As the deafening roar rose in that hall, I suddenly felt a deep calm, an inner silence. It felt that I was somehow tuning into something bigger than and beyond my fear. I became at one with those in the room, feeling their pain and suffering. I took a breath and surprised myself. I realised that I did have a choice: I could go on with the planned speech and defend the current institutional system of the Department, buying time, offering piecemeal solutions, negotiating our way out of the immediate predicament. Or I could step out of my comfort zone and become vulnerable: step into their space and identify with their pain and suffering. I realised intuitively that there was something bigger than the speech of the Department that needed to be said.

Without any plan to do so, I tuned in to a deeper source of energy and raised my hand to speak. Within a few minutes the room became silent as they stared at me with suspicion and distrust. I removed my jacket and placed it on a chair, pointed to it and said:

> There is the consultant, the mediator and facilitator but here I am. My name is Frederick Hölscher and yes, I am a white Afrikaner man. And yes, my people are the authors of apartheid, and yes, we have caused a lot of pain and harm to our society and...'

I continued to share my vulnerability, stripping away the façade of my white skin that had brought me so many privileges. I identified with their fear, and their frustration at being dominated by the white race that removed their freedom and their future. I related to their pain without any effort to justify and explain why we Afrikaners had done what we did. By this time a deathly silence had descended in the room. I still do not know where the courage came from to say what I said next:

> But there is one thing I disagree with you on. You believe the liberation struggle belongs only to black people but it also belongs to us white Afrikaners, we are part of it. We have our own liberation to go through. Liberation from a mind-set of exclusion and separation, a mindset of domination and control. We also need to be liberated from the stereotypes that keep us hostage, so we can see other people for who they really are.

I invited the students to help me and my people to become truly liberated.

As I spoke the air was punctured with a chant: 'Viva, Comrade Frederick, Viva! I realised that we had stepped, for a moment, into a new unity of hope. Not because we were in agreement, but because we were part of a deeper purpose: the freedom of humankind seeking for expression. We all realised we were fighting the same battle, the oppressed and the oppressor. Sadly, the Rector was not pleased with me as I was not successful in my negotiation to get him back at the helm. He informed me that my services would no longer be needed at his college.

In retrospect, I had lost my job but walked away from that day with a deep sense of liberation. One of being able to step out of my own 'stuckness' where I was preoccupied with defending and protecting my identity. I saw myself through the eyes of others without defence or fear. Although I was exposed, I was not intimidated. I became vulnerable as I stripped myself from the facades of superiority and pride and showed myself to those who had been painted as my fiercest enemies. I felt courage and strength when I found myself intuitively united with them in the deeper virtue of freedom and justice. I drew energy from a source beyond my own plans and skills. I realised that we were just different notes in a deeper symphony of life.

Four years later Nelson Mandela walked free, and he and FW de Klerk, the last apartheid president, were on their way to becoming Nobel Peace Prize winners. A triumph of openness in a world previously shaped by two trapped states of mind, locked in a deeply rooted conflict.

After the initial platform for a new unity was built by these two leaders, more people were needed with liberated minds to give shape to a new South Africa and build on the foundations of a deep sense of unity. Unfortunately, as we now know, those who took up the leadership mantle have struggled (or been unwilling) to build on the base created by Mandela and de Klerk.

A framework for understanding

To help understand how people learn and grow we use a framework of ego development, because in our definition of the ego, it is the shaper and driver of development. In Chapter 3 we described how leaders experience the downsides of ego intelligence when they become trapped in their personal ego needs. In this chapter we return to our discussion of the 'stuck' versus the 'benevolent' or liberated ego.

Ego development theory or EDT has fascinated many authors from Maslow[2] in the 1940s through numerous others in the 50s, 60s and 70s, to more recently Cook-Greuter (2000)[3] Graves (2005),[4] Torbert (2005),[5] Zohar (2012)[6] and Barrett (2014/2015)[7].

These theories explore how our behaviour is influenced by our conscious and unconscious ego needs which lie 'below the waterline', out of sight to others. Most ego stage theories see development as an evolutionary sequence of stages, each with expanding world views from birth to adulthood. They describe how growth occurs in a logical sequence. Later stages are reached by journeying through earlier stages. Once a stage has been traversed, it remains a part of the individual's response repertoire, even when more complex later stages are adopted. A person's stage of development influences what they need and become aware of: therefore, what they can describe, cultivate or influence. This is commonly referred to as levels of consciousness.

Healthy development increases our ability to deal with dualities and paradoxes, enabling a greater interactivity with the environment and lower defensiveness.

Ego development theories resonate with most people because we have experienced how our mindset shifts and evolves through childhood, the school system, adolescence and adulthood as we learn to deal with the dualities and paradoxes that present themselves in 'crucible moments' in our lives. From this perspective, biological development is one of the foundations of the development journey. There is merit in these models and they are supported by rigorous empirical research.

However, we challenge the linear thinking adopted by those who depict this development journey as a neat step by step journey from the first to the last stage. In our exploration of the three leadership intelligences we were initially tempted to outline a linear process of development from ego to eco to intuitive intelligence as the highest form of leadership development. However, we soon realised that this is idealistic and abandoned that linear concept of development. Instead we embrace a more reflexive approach that includes a constant interplay between the intelligences. Also, an intelligence is not necessarily linked to a specific stage of ego development. They all play out throughout our development journey as we explain in this chapter.

We therefore emphasise an important point raised by Susanne Cook-Greuter (1985, 2013)[8]. That these ego stages are 'idealisations' in that they describe the ideal outcome of healthy development for each increase of awareness and integration at a new level. No individual fits all the aspects of these descriptions; they serve only as a roadmap.

Our personal development journey is defined by the interplay between ourselves and our environment: how we make sense of and integrate the dualities and paradoxes that exist at each stage, from the very first stage to the last.

Despite the overall evolutionary direction of development, individuals move in *all* directions: horizontally within a development stage as they gain new skills and knowledge, as well as regressing to earlier sense-making stages when faced with crises or illness over long periods of time. Cook-Greuter's MAP psychometric[9] that measures an individual's stage of development found that responses seldom span over less than three of the ego stages, indicating a broad range of responses across the stages. She speaks about a person's 'centre of gravity' being the stage of ego maturity most accessed under ordinary circumstances (i.e. not in crises). When people 'regress' in a crisis, they will carry with them the insights and perspectives from the latest stage of their development and be able to bring those perspectives to whatever crises they are experiencing.

In Figure 6.1 below we show how the ego develops and matures using a model depicted in a similar way to 'babushkas': wooden Russian nesting dolls, where the bigger dolls contain a series of smaller and smaller dolls. It shows how the elements and ego needs from our early development stages as children are still present within us as adults (bigger doll), and how we move back and forth to them during our adult development journey, in reaction to contextual challenges we encounter.

Our ego needs from previous stages never completely disappear, but become less prominent if we are able to recognise and integrate the dualities or tensions inherent in ourselves at each of these stages.

This is the process the psychologist Carl Jung[10] called *Individuation* – how we deal with and integrate our unconscious urges and needs with our conscious reality: how this process gives definition to who we uniquely are and our personality. In this chapter we show how this process of individuation already starts at the earliest stages of our childhood development and how it plays out in our adult lives.

Drawing on our own experience and the work of Barrett, Erikson and others, the next section gives a brief overview of the evolutionary ego development journey linked to our biological and psychological development.

In the womb we have a complete sense of oneness with our mother. From the moment we are born and the umbilical cord is cut, our process of separation of the 'self' from others (our mother being the first) starts and the ego develops through various phases characterised by specific ego needs. We explore the stages 1–3 shown in the model below. Having explored these first three stages, we take a deeper look at the adult experience of individuation which then leads us to stages 4–6.

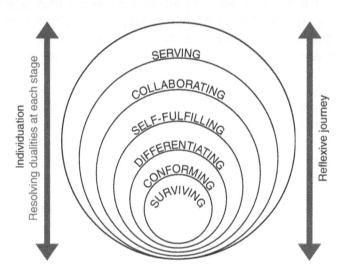

Figure 6.1 Stages of development

The first three stages (the general agreement)

The ego first develops through the expression of our most basic need for *survival*, to which we add *security* within an adult and organisational context (stage 1 – *surviving*). This is first experienced at age 0–2 years when any baby's first unconscious need is for food and protection. The baby is acutely aware of its needs for food but realises it needs other people to provide this food, so he or she finds ways to get people to pay attention e.g., by screaming. This then becomes the pattern of behaviour.

As adults we often experience this stage again when we are confronted with a crisis that threatens our security e.g., pandemics, disease and our own death.

The second level manifests itself as a need to *belong* and to be loved which makes us conform in order to fit in (stage 2 – *conforming*). This stage is first experienced around the ages of 2–8 years old. Children at this age need to feel a strong sense of family, routine, and love. They need to feel part of a 'tribe' that cares for them and their identity is defined as part of the tribe identity. This tribe could be a family, a team at work or even a sports team. They engage in sibling rivalry and become highly competitive in order to feel accepted by parents or friends. This then becomes a pattern of behaviour that defines their personality. Adults who experience this ego need will work hard to fit in or belong to a group and may be overly sensitive to rejection, or may compete with others in order to feel more accepted in their team.

The anthroposophical philosophy of the Rudolf Steiner[11] (Waldorf) schooling system is designed to match the phases of ego development in children. For example, between the ages of 6 to 13 years, children remain with one teacher and class over their first seven years of schooling. This provides a sense of a caring "family" when most needed in the child's development. From high school, around age 13, teenagers in this schooling system are encouraged towards higher independence and to discover their unique sense of self and talents.

This plays into the third stage which shows up as our need for a special status (stage 3 – *differentiating*), to be different, to stand out, be special, where a strong desire for self-expression starts to play out. Teenagers need to struggle with the confusion inherent in finding their identity in the world. They need to release their dependency on their family's approval, which can be quite traumatic for parents. This can be seen in the way teenagers start to express their uniqueness through the way they dress, talk and behave. They need to challenge the world (and their parents) in a quest to find their unique voice.

So, like the Russian nesting dolls, although these needs first manifest in our early years of development, they remain with us to a greater or lesser extent as adults and become part of our adult development journey. As discussed in Chapter 3, our ego is an essential part of ourselves and it never leaves us. We inevitably and continually re-experience the panic of survival (stage 1), the need for acceptance and fear of rejection (stage 2), and the need for recognition and status (stage 3) throughout our adult lives. We are constantly moving between these stages as a response to the challenges facing us at any given time but we approach each challenge with the mindset or consciousness of the most developed stage (our centre of gravity).

At each stage of development, we are challenged with specific paradoxes or dualities. For example, babies need to learn 'who to trust versus who to distrust', teenagers need to struggle with 'identity versus confusion' etc. Each of these stages therefore plays an important role in our development.

The way in which we master and integrate these paradoxes influences the kind of person we uniquely become, our personality.

As we master and integrate the dualities at each stage, we are able to expand our consciousness or awareness.

Each stage also has a shadow or downside which emerges when we become 'stuck' in a specific stage and ego need e.g. leaders or politicians who are not able to move beyond their need for recognition or status display all kinds of competitive and narcissistic behaviour. Many people never develop beyond stage 3 (differentiating), expressed as the need for status and recognition, as can be seen with many senior leaders in organisations.

Our research uncovered insights into how these ego needs impact on leadership approach and style.

We found that effective ego intelligent leaders (with a mature or benevolent ego) understand their own ego driven needs and are then able to relate to and tap into the ego needs of others.

They satisfy them by providing what is needed and use their own ego strengths to serve instead of dictate. For example, providing the team with a sense of security (your job is safe here), belonging (we are a great team and you are part of us) or differentiation (you are the best consultant in this team). However, when leaders themselves get stuck in their own unfulfilled ego needs they tend to demonstrate the shadow side of ego leadership e.g., greed, egotism, narcissism, or silo mentality.

The table below describes the gifts and shadows for the first three ego development stages:

Ego stages	1. Surviving (Need for security and survival)	2. Conforming (Need for acceptance and belonging)	3. Differentiating (Need for recognition and survival)
Description	The need to feel secure and safe	The need for inclusion, to belong or to 'fit in', could include our need for psychological safety	The need to stand out, to be special or different
Gift (related to the workplace)	Staying power/ tenure Awareness of own needs Dependability Reliability	Conforming to the rules/team player Emotional connection They promote a sense of care and 'family'	Ruthlessly driven Hard worker/ achiever in order to prove their differentiation to others, especially to the leadership team
Shadow (related to the workplace)	Disempowering beliefs like "I am not safe" or "I will not make it" leading to: • Others are there to fulfil my needs • Obsession with job security • Resistance to change • Inflexibility • May become aggressive in defending one's territory	Disempowering beliefs like "I do not belong here", "they don't care about me, "I don't fit", "I feel rejected" leading to: • An over-sensitivity to not being included e.g. in emails, meetings or projects • Withdrawing, not speaking up • Pleasing others and sacrificing own needs in order to 'fit in'	Disempowering beliefs like "I am not recognised enough" "I am not good enough" leading to: • An over-reaction to perceived lack of recognition or status • Managing upwards to look good to the boss - self-promotion • Bringing down colleagues who may be perceived as competition or a threat

The stories below from our own lives and those of our research participants show how these ego needs typically manifest in the workplace. As you read these, consider your own needs, which of these resonate with you?

Stage 1. Surviving: the need for survival and security

George explained how he was feeling fearful and panicky because his organisation was rationalising to save costs by removing layers in the hierarchy and moving towards flatter structures of self-organising teams. This also meant giving more autonomy to teams to establish how they define their roles and work together. Many of the team members were excited about this new freedom and empowerment. However, having gone through a painful redundancy experience with his previous employer, George was at a point of his life where financial and job security was very important, and he perceived this change as a threat to his security. He needed to know that he had a clear role within the organisational structure for the foreseeable future, and needed it be well structured and not fluid. Instead of feeling excited about the opportunities presented by a more empowered way of working, George was emotionally paralysed and filled with fear because of his strong need for financial security and survival.

Stage 2. Conforming: the need for acceptance and belonging

During her interview with us, Marlene talked about the "gnawing feeling in the pit of her stomach" in team meetings. She said she has great ideas to contribute but mostly does not share them because she feels a lack of acceptance and belonging in her team. She said "I am not one of them. They are all extroverted men, they speak loudly, they have their own jokes, and they appear so self-assured and confident...I want to fit in but conforming to their ways is just not me!" This insecurity is aggravated by her tendency towards introversion. Marlene is an experienced leader whose ideas and insights would certainly be of benefit to the team. However, they will not be shared until she is able to deal with her need for acceptance and overcome her fear of rejection and exclusion. Interestingly, this does not play out in other areas of her life where she feels successful and confident to contribute. It is definitely contextual.

We all have (to a greater or lesser extent) these needs for security, belonging and differentiation. These needs are a natural part of our development journey, and their intensity differs depending on the context e.g., work versus family versus community. As we mature into adulthood, our response to dealing with these natural ego needs is found in becoming more self-aware and finding ways to accept, integrate and hopefully transcend these needs. Sometimes however, when childhood wounds have remained with us, these needs become quite strongly rooted within us through time and are hard to change. Some refer to these as our 'pain bodies' (what we call the black widow spider). These 'pain bodies' become part of who we are, and a source of energy that drives us.

The next story is an example of this.

Stage 3. Differentiating: the need for recognition and status

Peter was the second child. His elder brother was a great sportsman, popular at school and generously praised by their father. Peter was always in the background trying to get his father's attention. He went to university and became a medical doctor, always working hard to get the recognition he craved but did not receive from his father. He developed great people skills with his patients and managed to get all the attention and recognition he so craved from his patients and his staff. Throughout his life, whether he acknowledged it or not, Peter was unconsciously competing with his brother, and craving the recognition from his father. This strong need for differentiation and status made him very successful, and he built up a formidable medical practice and became very wealthy. However, he told us that he could "never relax and smell the roses" because he felt the need to keep achieving in order to stand out (differentiate). Although, in adult life, he had become much more successful than his brother, his black widow never left him. He became addicted to the recognition of others and needing to be the best.

He and a few colleagues started a medical organisation where he was initially well received because of his charisma and innovative ways of doing things (again his need for status and to be seen as different). However, when he was challenged to align himself to the group's vision and strategy, he struggled. His colleagues confronted him and told him to "tow the line and fit in with the group's way". His need for differentiation was severely threatened. In a rage, Peter unexpectedly broke ranks, giving no notice, and started his own business where he could be 'in charge'. He took a large number of faithful patients with him because he was their hero. This breakaway from colleagues and friends caused significant emotional damage and a breaking down of trust. His colleagues were left feeling pressurised to choose between following him or staying with the larger organisation. Half of them decided to follow Peter causing even further pain and disruption to the organisation.

Let's delve deeper into why the ego gets stuck and how the 'black widow spider' operates.

The stuck ego and the black widow spider

Imagine a web with a dangerous black widow spider sitting in the centre. The spider represents an unresolved ego need or issue, for example our ego need for belonging. The spider spins its web in our brains through a process called cognitive mapping. This web can become quite extensive through the accumulation of reinforcing negative experiences. The more threads are spun through accumulated emotional experiences, the stronger the web. In our example above, Peter became successful and received many accolades, yet this was not enough to quench his ego need for differentiation and recognition: the web became bigger and stronger.

These spiders react fast if a strand of their web is even gently touched. For example, just a sniff of feedback, linked to our black widow, may lead to an over-reaction by our spider. Marlene (from the example above) explained how her first reaction, when she is not included in an invitation to a meeting, triggered her self-talk of: "I am not good enough" and "they don't need me". This created stress to the extent that she was struggling to sleep at night because of her continuous ruminating about it. Her black widow spider lurks within her stage 2 ego 'conforming': the need for acceptance and belonging. It not only disturbs her own emotional state but also impacts on her colleagues when she retaliates and starts criticising and gossiping about those who she feels are excluding her. Wonderful people may instantly turn into emotional monsters when you awaken their black widows!

The apparent success of many senior leaders and CEOs is driven by excessive ego or narcissistic tendencies – as in Peter's case when he faced the choice between aligning with his colleagues or satisfying the craving of his black widow. It seems that the black widow often gets its way. This is one of the reasons the ego has such a bad name in leadership – leaders fail to make friends with their black widows in order to be able to use their ego strengths constructively. In other words, their behaviour becomes driven by their black widow – whether it is helpful or not.

Collective ego

An interesting phenomenon surfaces when the ego is in operation at a collective or group level. It can occur when an individual feels a strong sense of belonging to a group and the ego's needs for belonging are satisfied as it identifies itself with the group. This identification of the ego with the collective belief system can be so strong that the individual sees no difference between himself or herself and the group and is prepared to sacrifice much for the group's ideals, sometimes even their own life, as is the case with suicide bombers. This is where activists often find energy and expression for their cause. In a sense, the collective ego becomes the hero as it assumes the appearance of greatness.

There is a complete acceptance of the shared values and little toleration of opposition or challenge from the outside. Consider politicians, some CEO's, religions or any activist group. The collective ego becomes the judge of what is acceptable, and what is right and wrong.

The same thing happens in adolescence. When the adolescent's need for differentiation finds its home in a group that differentiates itself in some way, for example 'the cool kids' or 'the nerds', it has quite an impact on how they behave.

This is where many leaders and politicians find themselves today – emboldened by their sense of righteousness within their 'tribe'. They use positive descriptions like 'America first' and rely on self-determination and patriotism to impose boundaries around them, leading to silos within organisations and nationalism within countries.

Personal reflection (on the first three stages)

Where do you find yourself within these various ego stages? Take a moment to consider these questions:

- What is most important to you about your work environment? What would make you want to stay with an organisation?

- Related to the first question, where do you find yourself today on the ego stage development framework? Why do you say so?

- Are you able to identify your black widow spider? What does it say to you? Remember, the black widow often shows up as an inner critic voice e.g., "you don't belong here" or "you aren't good enough"

- Think of a metaphor that symbolises your black widow. What energy does this metaphor hold for you?

The adult experience of individuation

The question of whether we can transcend (or get rid of) our black widow spiders has been the topic of scholars for many years. Let's return to the individuation process. We described how, as children, we master each stage by learning how to get our needs met by manipulating or influencing parents, caregivers or friends. These early patterns of behaviour help form or individuate us in the world as children and may remain with us for many years into adulthood.

For adults, usually from about the age of 20, the individuation process is a different experience. It enables us to become more self-aware (conscious) of our (sometimes unconscious) immature ego needs and black widows. We start to notice how our needs and fears around security/safety (stage 1), belonging (stage 2) or status (stage 3) can trip us up by driving unhelpful behaviour e.g., undue competitiveness in the workplace or playing up to the boss in our craving for recognition. For example, in Frederick's story, in that crucible moment, he became acutely aware of his and others need for safety. It took a great deal of courage to step out of that fear and to individuate himself by establishing his identity as comrade or 'co-sufferer' and to show empathy for their pain. This then helped the crowd to 'see him' as a person, as individuated from his white, apartheid labelled, tribe.

Individuation helps us become aware that we are more than, or bigger than, our immature ego needs and that these needs do not have to define who we are.

We are then more able to 'tame' and reframe our ego needs and even release some of our fear-driven ego needs which means that they have less of a grip on our behaviour. The black widow spider now becomes more like an annoying neighbour, popping her head over the fence when you do not want to see her, rather than a black widow spider!

This requires us to spend some time thinking about ourselves, to do some introspection: learning to know, accept and integrate our ego needs as different parts of ourselves. This process of individuation opens up a beautiful space within us as it enables us to 'see beyond ourselves' and to add value to others, tapping into our sense of meaning and purpose. Or as Barrett (2015)[12] explains it, "to focus on our soul needs as opposed to our deficiency needs." This brings a tremendous sense of emotional freedom. We lessen our need for external validation and start to accept ourselves for who we are – and who we are *not*.

Jung also explains how in the first three stages we *think* we know who we are but that it is a rather one-sided sense of certainty or illusion because we are lacking the self-awareness that comes with the adult experience of individuation. In the first three stages we do not notice or pay attention to the inherent tensions and oppositions between the conscious self we portray to the world (I am kind and loving) and the unconscious, darker parts of ourselves (I am capable of deep hatred and anger), for example. The ancient Taoist symbol of yin and yang represents the balance or harmony of these opposites. Yang is the sunny light side while yin represents the shadowy side.

Jung explains how, if we do not learn to address these tensions, we deny their existence and then repress or push them out of consciousness. But repressing does not eliminate the opposites or the tension itself. It only makes them more destructive in our psyche by strengthening our shadows. It is not easy but this is part of the goal of the individuation process. It can be a difficult process for the ego that has become entrenched in the certainty of its own identity and style or even in the identity of the tribe.

The adult experience of individuation thus indicates an ego maturity where we are aware of and able to embrace and integrate these tensions (yin and yang) within ourselves.

In this process we learn to 'know ourselves' more fully and have less of a need for external validation.

The process of individuation opens us up to different kinds of motivational drivers that are more rooted in focusing *beyond* satisfying our ego's needs for security, belonging or differentiation.

These include self-fulfillment (also called self-actualisation by Maslow) (stage 4) which means to find a bigger sense of meaning and purpose by more fully living out our talents and potential, often experienced in our late 30s or 40s. Some people make dramatic career changes at this stage of life as they realise that they are not getting any younger and question whether their current job will enable them to live out their potential or give them any sense of meaning and purpose going forward. This is often referred as the mid-life crisis.

Colin tells his story...

After studying hotel management at the College of Food and Domestic Arts in Birmingham U.K. (now known as University College Birmingham), I chose to become a chef rather than go into hotel management. I set off on a learning journey, starting with a year in Germany followed by eight years in France.

Being a head chef is an interesting challenge. It is personal (individual reputations are at stake), requires an exhaustive technical knowledge, the practical/craft skills to apply that knowledge, an ability to motivate people to work long hours, under pressure, in uncomfortable conditions and a commitment to the highest standards of quality – on time and on budget – every day! In many ways it is perfect ground for ego intelligent leadership.

My first experience, apart from working in hotels and restaurants in and around Birmingham as a student, was a year spent at a prestigious international hotel in Germany. Although most successful head chefs are not the hot-tempered tyrants caricatured in reality television shows – this one was! Exhausting, hectic lunch and dinner services were sometimes followed by ritual humiliation as staff were made to stand in a line while the 'chef' ranted emotionally about how awful we were and how we did not deserve such a leader as he. He was credited with maintaining the high standards recognised internationally but for me was a deeply flawed man who was living out his demons in public.

At first, I found this ritual frustrating and demotivating, watching this man's black widow spider spinning a web around us. As a young man I had some admiration for this famous chef but I also realised that I could not allow myself to be caught up in his web. I had to take some distance and be true to myself. Although I could not have articulated it as such at the time, this was a test for my self-actualisation and individuation. I became like the reeds in a storm, allowing the force of his ego needs to blow over me.

Over time I realised that the kitchen worked largely despite, not because of, him. One of the sous chefs (deputy) was actually the orchestra leader. He was a quiet man who rarely raised his voice but exuded what is best described as air an of natural authority. This clear 'liberated ego' leadership approach was what motivated people and ensured the effective operation of the kitchen.

I found myself becoming curious about my own underlying assumptions about leadership. With hindsight I realise that my leadership approach, as I worked my way to being a head chef myself, was based on ego intelligence – a liking for structure, clarity, organisation, predictability and expecting loyalty in return for support. And this is still my underlying preference today although I believe I have added an ability to work as an eco intelligent leader. I still struggle with intuition although I (usually!) value it in others.

Stage 5 (collaborating) is characterised by our need to make a difference in the world through integrating with others, striving to make a difference to something bigger than ourselves. We have a need to be part of a bigger ecosystem with like-minded people, together making a difference in the world. We realise that we cannot and do not want to do this on our own. We become very aware of the interdependencies between us and others and place emphasis on how to collaborate with others. We lose our appetite for competition and showing off how special and different we are.

We also become aware of our need to 'give back' to the world and to others, and often engage in mentoring and coaching at this stage.

Sharon describes how this played out in her life:

During my 20s and 30s I had a great job as HR leader in VW and Audi for ten years. I enjoyed this role because it satisfied my need for security and belonging in my early career, as part of a multi-national, where I was valued and had some good friends (stage 2).

In my mid-thirties I experienced a phase of acute dissatisfaction with this role. I felt that I needed to establish my unique voice in the world and to create 'my own thing' (need for differentiation stage 3). So, I joined a small consulting organisation, and only a year later felt that I could be even more independent and that I really did need my independence. I resigned, and my partner and I started our own small consulting practice called "Independent Network Consultants" which lasted for the next 15 years of my life. My motivation was underpinned by my need for differentiation (stage 3), wanting to develop a unique offering and IP (intellectual property) in the world, that would bring a competitive advantage. I found myself indignant and upset when others 'stole' our IP and made money from it.

This small venture kept me happy and satisfied for a long time. However, around the age of 50, I noticed a shift happening in me. I started feeling a strong need to join a bigger organisation, and I was struggling to understand why. For the first time, I felt isolated and lonely. Also, I was realising how limited our little operation was. We could not really make a difference in the bigger scheme of things. This need felt very different to when I first joined the motor industry as HR leader. It was not driven by a need for belonging or security, but rather by a need for integration and collaboration (stage 5) with like-minded others, which would enable me/us to reach more people, and make a bigger difference in the world. The opportunity to emigrate to the UK and the job offer from Ashridge business school all happened synchronously at this time, and have met these needs beautifully. Today I often surprise myself in the way I now respond to challenges. For example, I have lost my need to protect my IP and nowadays freely offer it to anyone interested! The writing of this book is another example of how my need to integrate and collaborate with my colleagues has found expression in something tangible and special. I am reminded of the African concept of Ubuntu which means 'I am because We are'.

Stage 6 (service) emerges when we more fully identify ourselves as 'one' with a bigger whole, and realise that separation is an illusion. This is referred to as 'unity' consciousness by Ken Wilber[13]. We become focused on how we can be 'of service' to this bigger whole. We experience a greater humility and perspective on our own importance. A wise teacher once said to Sharon, "in my old age I have realised there are only two things that are enduring and important, the quality of my relationships, and being of service to others".

Here is the story of Heinrich, a friend and colleague:

For most of his adult life, Heinrich had been successful because of his ability to 'sell' in his role as salesman. People said that he could sell ice to an Eskimo! He was strongly motivated to make money in order to please his wife and make his children proud of their neighbourhood, private school and home. In his mid-life, he had achieved significant material wealth and reached the position of top achiever in his organisation.

Heinrich's life is very different today. At the age of 72, he has completely lost his drive to sell and to make money, even though he is not particularly wealthy. He is far more interested in how he can help others to establish themselves, and does not expect special recognition or accolades, in fact he avoids them. In a conversation he reflected "My wish is that everything I do during my last years on this planet would add value in some way to others. I don't need to be rich or famous! When I see others using my ideas or advice, and how it enhances their success, it makes me very happy."

As mentioned at the start of this chapter, although these ego needs may initially be first experienced as part of a psychological and biological development journey, the adult experience of them is not a linear phenomenon, rather a contextual one. For example, as we write in November 2020 the COVID-19 virus pandemic is having a huge impact on peoples' lives all around the world. Many people are obsessed with survival and financial security (the first stage), whilst at the same time sorely missing the contact with their communities (need for belonging, stage 2), and simultaneously not wanting to lose sight of their bigger purpose during these times (stage 5). We however recognise that the type of awareness or consciousness that an adult brings to a crisis will be indicative of their "centre of gravity" or stage of development prior to the crisis. For example, someone at the collaboration stage of development will approach the crisis situation with wisdom and empathy whilst someone at the survival stage may approach it with a frenetic sense of panic.

We also suggest that biological age is becoming less of a factor in how quickly generations are developing through these stages. For example, the consciousness of generations Y and Z appear to be different to previous generations. As we said in Chapter 1, young people are more connected and motivated by things like organisational purpose and planetary concerns than were the babyboomers when they were young. This must have an impact on how and when they experience the development stages. We believe that the so-called ego deficiency needs are therefore playing out differently in the current world of 'abundance' in the information age. More research into this would be good to see.

The impact of crucible moments in personal transformation

As leaders shared their personal journeys with us, we observed that the impetus for the transformation of their leadership approach was often prompted by 'crucible' or defining moments in their lives; moments that nudged them out of their comfort zone to experiment with new ways of being and leading, as beautifully told by this CEO:

Asked if he had always led with his strong eco style he said, "No, I wasn't like this before." He further explained, "I was educated to strive to be at the top in a highly competitive work environment, told that you have to be in control, measuring everything and taking strong top-down action. These became the leadership characteristics I strived for - and I became a control freak. As a teenager I was strongly influenced by my father who was continuously pushing me to be perfect: 90% was not good enough. This turned me into a hard-driving perfectionist".

The upside of this perfectionism was that he pushed himself relentlessly. However, this need for perfectionism brought continuous insecurity about not being good enough. As he matured, he increasingly felt a sense of dissatisfaction and a sense that "something is missing" leading to unhappiness and dissatisfaction.

About five years ago this leader started working with a coach who helped him realise that, in his words, "For almost 45 years, I had not understood why I was functioning the way I was!"

His breakthrough 'crucible moment' came when he realised that his unhappiness was rooted in the power of his ego needs for control and recognition (stage 3) on the one hand and need for acceptance (stage 2) on the other: "I realised I was a control freak and a love junkie." The recognition of the duality within him was the turning point. It created an internal dissonance that became unbearable. This pain prompted him to explore alternative ways of being and leading. With the help of his coach he started exploring how to integrate these opposite needs and how both had a positive value for him. He started experimenting with self-acceptance, trusting his leaders more, letting go of control and following his intuition more. His board now describe him as a well-rounded leader, deeply caring but also able to stretch boundaries and take risks.

The 'how' of individuation

Next, let's explore how both this process of ego development and individuation relates to ego, eco and intuitive intelligence.

We do this by outlining three aspects or phases within the process of individuation:

Meta awareness

This term was originally coined by developmental psychologist John Flavell (1977)[14] as "thinking about our thinking". It refers to the uniquely human capacity to step back or take distance from oneself and one's ego, and then to simply notice with curiosity instead of fear. Some describe this as stepping from the dance floor, where you are active and engaged, onto the balcony, to observe yourself dancing. We quieten our active minds to simply become aware of our thoughts, body sensations, feelings, our reactions, and the voice of the black widow spider saying, "you are not safe enough, good enough, or special enough".

This also means becoming aware of the tensions or paradoxes within ourselves in a particular moment. For example, "I am noticing that I am needing to feel included *and* at the same time I want to be free to do what I want."

Meta awareness is probably one of the most powerful skills you can master in life as it opens up a space that enables you to shift from your automatic black widow *reactions* to defend, attack or withdraw, towards being able to *respond* 'choicefully'.

Meta awareness makes us "response-able" (responsible).

This might mean you shift from arrogance (I know what you should do) towards vulnerability (I am not sure, could we explore this together?). Meta awareness enables the second condition within the individuation process, to bring coherence.

Bringing integration (coherence) – eco intelligence

The first key is *acceptance* (and love) of the different parts of yourself and the acknowledgement that all parts are there to serve you in some way. For example, in the story above – "how can my control freak and my love junkie serve me?

Secondly, using our eco intelligent ability to *integrate* different or opposing parts (dualities or paradoxes) within ourselves. In other words, coming to an appreciation of the dualities that are an essential part of who you are – I am disciplined *and* I am a wild child, I am loving *and I* am angry, I am strong *and* I am weak. When the black widow hijacks us through the voice of the inner critic, e.g., "I am not good enough", we are able, through our meta awareness, to notice and catch ourselves in the moment…ah…there's my black widow again…hello Harry!

Can we fully accept that this aspect is a part of ourselves and that there are other parts also, and that it is ok? Both have a positive intention for us. In other words, we acknowledge the yin yang within us, the light side and the shadow side.

The key is to learn to replace *fear* with *curiosity.*

"Ah, there I go again beating myself up, how interesting. I wonder what this is trying to show me?" And so your black widow becomes your teacher instead of your master.

This frees us up to choose another response in the moment – to become response-able, e.g., "this is my issue (black widow), not theirs…so how can I respond differently in this moment?"

Eco intelligence is therefore not only our ability to integrate diverse people and ideas across organisational boundaries but is also our ability to achieve an *inner* integration or coherence. This opens up a space within us for an experience of wholeness.

Sense of wholeness: intuitive intelligence

Many people struggle to find their full potential. We mentioned in our discussion in Chapter 4 that intuitive intelligence has, at its root, a sense of connection to the bigger whole or oneness – not as an end goal but as the point of departure. It is the realisation that we are all 'one' but have become separated because of the powerful working of the ego which creates this separation because of its preoccupation with clear identity and boundaries: 'this is me, as separate from you'.

However, the ego has never forgotten about this wholeness (experienced pre-birth) hence its need to expand its boundaries to include everything into its own sphere of influence. In the earlier stages of ego development, the ego tends to disregard or eliminate ideas or people who do not fit. They are disregarded or separated, until the ego discovers that separation is an illusion and that we are all connected in some way.

This realisation brings a sense of humility to the ego and it loses some of its drive for security, acceptance or differentiation.

This journey can be painful and beautiful at the same time, and is often sparked by some crucible moment in our development journey.

People who allow this sense of wholeness to mature in them, realise that they will never get rid of the ego and its needs but that this is all part of the bigger whole that is 'me'. They also realise that the thing that is tripping them up is often a universal or collective issue, as one leader said, 'Welcome to humanity. I am dealing with this fear of rejection on behalf of humanity, it does not only belong to me, I carry this with and for so many!'

We believe that we all came into the world with this sense of wholeness and that throughout our lives, we lose it, gain it, lose it, etc. as we go through moments of connection or moments of feeling lost and separated in a fragmented world. But it is always there, calling us to develop our ability to deal with paradox.

It is often when our mind seizes up and our emotions are numbed during turbulent times that we have to dig deeper and find something that reminds us that we are not alone but part of something much bigger that seeks expression through us. As Parker Palmer (2004)[15] said, "Wholeness does not mean perfection: it means embracing brokenness as an integral part of life".

This chapter in a nutshell

Our ego is our unique sense of self in the world. The development of the ego can be characterised by a range of ego stages each with its unique ego needs. The first three stages are characterised by our need for survival, acceptance and differentiation. When we struggle to integrate these ego needs, we experience their shadow side (the black widow spider). These black widow spiders tend to unconsciously trip us up as leaders, often showing up to others as an inflated ego, silo mentality, managing upwards to receive praise, ruthlessly competing and narcissistic leadership behaviour.

Our development involves the maturation of the ego which Jung describes as the process of individuation. This is not a linear process but carries on throughout our lives as we come to grips with the human paradoxes and dualities in different situations, from our childhood right through to our death. It starts with a self-awareness of our ego needs and black widow spiders. This self-awareness helps us to individuate, which means to recognise, accept and then integrate these paradoxes, and to enquire into who we really are independent of the culture and environment in which we were raised. This ability to integrate the paradoxes at the various stages of development is characteristic of eco intelligence. Extended beyond the boundaries of separation, our eco intelligence integrates our intuitive intelligence which is our sense of connection to the bigger whole or 'oneness'.

Reflection and application

We end this chapter by offering a simple (but not easy) reframing process we facilitate in the classroom to help leaders to use their ego, eco and intuitive intelligence in an integrative way to deal with difficult challenges facing them due to the dominance of their ego stuckness or black widow spiders.

We encourage you to try it for yourself and with your team. The process is an adaptation of the 'three perceptual positions' often used in NLP (neurolinguistic process) coaching.

These positions will help you to step back (meta awareness) and to *reframe* how you view and approach a difficult leadership situation. These difficulties could include a disagreement between yourself and others, a challenging staff member or even stakeholder group. It aims to help you to gain self-awareness, show empathy and understanding, and to gain fresh insights about the situation.

Figure 6.2 Reframing process

Step 1: Using your Ego Intelligence (step into)

Set up three chairs to symbolise three positions in a shape of the three circles in the diagram. Sit on chair 1. In this chair you are totally associated to your own experience of the situation. You see it and hear it through your own filters. Sit quietly for a moment and access the full extent of your thoughts, feelings, needs. Verbalise...I think.., I feel..., I need..., and when I overdo this thing I become...this kind of person. (We often ask people to imagine holding a sword because it is in this position that you defend your truth and are prepared to fight for your point of view). Here you access your ego needs, your ego strength with all its boundaries and your black widow.

Step 2: using your eco intelligence (step out)

Get up and step out (leaving the sword behind on the first chair) into position 2 – the position of the 'other'. Here you need the *courage* to bracket your own view and feelings and to viscerally become the other (person or stakeholder or even organisation), just for a moment. Now using the first-person language of "I" for the other person, verbalise...I think., I feel..., I need... and when I overdo this thing, I become ... (this kind of person/stakeholder/organisation). We often ask people to hold (or imagine) holding a magnifying glass in position 2 because it is in this position that you become *curious* about their truth. Here you are able to empathise with the other and the aim is to *understand* their position (not necessarily to agree with it). Here you use your eco intelligence as you explore positions beyond your own within the ecosystem.

Step 3: using your intuitive intelligence (step up)

Stepping up is most difficult as it involves *taking distance* and drawing on your *meta awareness* and your intuitive intelligence (sensing beyond the boundaries of the situation). Make sure the third chair is far enough away from the other to ensure you take emotional distance. Ask yourself, 'Who is the wisest person I know?', and for a moment become that person. Have a look at the other two positions (yours and theirs), and simply start to notice with curiosity. Ask "what is really going on here? "What are they needing?" And finally, "What advice would I give them?"

Step back into position 1

With this wisdom from your intuitive self step back into first position and ask yourself, "So with this wisdom, what is the very first step I will take? When will I take it? Who will I involve?"

The learning is a lifelong journey. Be aware that you may find that just as you feel you have had a breakthrough, you may start all over again. We wish you many breakthroughs!

Notes

1 Covey, S. (1989) The 7 Habits of Highly Effective People, *Simon and Schuster*, New York.
2 Maslow, Abraham H. (1943) A theory of human motivation. *Psychological Review* 50: 370–396.
3 Cook-Greuter, S. R. (2000) Mature ego development: A gateway to ego transcendence. *Journal of Adult Development* 47(4): 227.
  Cook-Greuter, S. R. (2013) Nine Levels of Increasing Embrace in Ego Development. Adapted and expanded from Cook-Greuter, S. R. (1985) A detailed description of the successive stages of ego-development. Revised Dec. 2013.
4 Graves, C. W. (2005) The Never-Ending Quest: A Treatise on an Emergent Cyclica, *ECLET Publishing*, Santa Barbara, CA.
5 Torbert, R. and Rooke, D. (2005) Seven Transformations of Leadership. *Harvard Business Review* 83(4): 66–76.
6 Zohar, D. and Marshall, I. (2012) Spiritual Intelligence: The Ultimate Intelligence, *Bloomsbury*, London.
7 Barrett, R. (2014) The Values Driven Organisation, Routledge, New York and Abingdon.
8 Cook-Greuter, S. R. (2013) Nine levels of increasing embrace in ego development. Adapted and expanded from Cook-Greuter, S. R. (1985) A detailed description of the successive stages of ego-development. Revised Dec. 2013.
9 http://www.cook-greuter.com/SCTi-MAPForm.htm
10 Jung, C. G. (1961) Erinnerungen, Traume, Gedanken (Memories Dreams, Reflections), *Random House Inc.*, New York.
11 https://www.waldorfeducation.org/waldorf-education/rudolf-steiner-the-history-of-waldorf-education
12 Barrett, R. (2015) The Metrics of Human Consciousness, *Lulu Publishing Services*, Morrisville, North Carolina.
13 Wilber, K. (2000) Integral Psychology: Consciousness, Spirit, Psychology, Therapy, *Shambhala*, Boston, MA.
14 Flavell, J. H. (1977) Cognitive Development, *Prentice Hall*, London.
15 Palmer, J. P. (2004) A Hidden Wholeness. The Journey Towards the Undivided Life. *Jossey-Bass*, San Francisco, CA.

Chapter 7

Leadership and cultural agility

Cultural agility is the ability to hold the paradox between stability and flexibility

Culture and leadership: two sides of a coin

In this chapter we explore different views of culture and describe the characteristics of an agile culture. We show leadership and culture as two sides of the same coin, then look at how leaders deal with their sense of cultural fit or 'misfit'. We outline how ego, eco and intuitive intelligences are as much a part of culture as they are of leadership and how these intelligences can be used by leaders to either preserve or evolve culture, and more specifically to build cultural agility.

What is culture?

The cultural identity of any collective, for example teams, organisations, countries or regions, is made up of shared assumptions about how things work and how things should be done. These underlying (often unconscious) assumptions lead to shared values which in turn drive behaviours. These behaviours become 'the way we do things around here' and are often beyond question, with no real understanding of where they originated. Challenging these behaviours can create a strong reaction as people feel their world is being destabilised or disoriented. The most vocal challengers to cultures are often the first to be shown the door. It is in human nature to want to eliminate the most disruptive people, those who do not 'fit in'. It is also part of human nature to want to bring in more people that fit well, to reinforce the culture. Repeat these two behaviours over time and culture becomes homogeny, even if everyone still believes that the culture values diversity!

The cry in the new world of work is for cultural agility, and many large corporate dinosaurs are knocking at the doors of business schools to help them become more structurally and culturally agile. "Help us become faster and more responsive to this fast-changing world."

We suggest that agile cultures have three defining features:

- agile cultures do not get stuck in a 'blueprint' mindset
- agile cultures are tuned into and are highly responsive to the bigger context

- agile cultures respond to the underlying paradoxes in an organisation

Let us take a look at each of these in turn.

Agile cultures do not get stuck in a blueprint mindset

One of the main shifts we identified in Chapter 2 is from *blueprint* to *process* thinking. Organisations often talk about the recipes or blueprints that have gotten them to where they are today and to which they account their success. Many large consulting companies use the term 'blueprint' within their transformational interventions. These recipes will be a mix of formalised elements such as products, processes and patents, and informal elements such as attitudes, behaviours and actions. Sometimes, however, the more successful the organisation, the more firmly the recipes become solidified or 'baked in' the culture. This makes change more difficult – even in the face of apparently incontrovertible evidence showing the need for change, for example, Kodak, BlackBerry, Nokia.

Sadly, these recipes of past success often become stumbling blocks for future success. What leaders often do is search for the new blueprint that will take them to future success. This keeps them trapped in in a continuous cycle of 'blueprint hopping'. The quest for transformation or change is therefore often couched in a search for a new 'recipe'.

We believe that the key lies not in defining the new recipe or destination but in the *process* of culture creation.

In our research we drew on the widely read work of Frederic Laloux (2014)[1] 'Reinventing Organisations' and his definitions of changing cultural paradigms described in Table 7.1. Laloux uses different colours to describe how human consciousness evolves in stages from red to teal which are often sparked by significant events, e.g., digital disruption, a radical competitor (and in our day, COVID-19), etc., that change how we see things 'suddenly'. This is reflected in the organisational culture.

Humanity evolves in stages. We are not like trees that grow continuously. We evolve by sudden transformations, like a caterpillar
that becomes a butterfly or a tadpole a frog.

Frederic Laloux (2014)

The following table should be read from the bottom (red) to the top
(teal) demonstrating the evolutionary stages.

Table 7.1 Laloux's types of organisational consciousness (adapted)

Types of organisational consciousness and key theme	Defining features
Teal (collaborate)	Takes the best from orange and green: Organisation as a self-organising network of teams, promoting wholeness (each person bringing their whole self to work), and 'evolutionary purpose' (holding the purpose lightly as it constantly evolves because of who is evolving it)
Green (care)	Focus on living out humanistic values (democracy, environment, inclusion) and creating a culture of empowerment to boost morale. Focus on stakeholders' value versus shareholder value, and being purpose-led
Orange (compete)	Characterised by competition and shareholder value, with the goal being to 'win' (beat the competition). Management by objectives, but with freedom to act and be innovative and to be entrepreneurial (as long as the objectives are achieved) sometimes 'at all costs', sacrificing people and morale
Amber (conform)	Formal roles within a hierarchical pyramid. Top down control via compliance to rules and regulations. High reliance on policies and procedures to provide the guidelines for acceptable behaviour
Red (control)	Cultures characterised by command and control practices. The exercising of power and fear to get people to comply. Creates a sense of dependency on the leader for direction

Although Laloux is clear that we should refrain from idealising the one over another, he defines the 'evolutionary Teal' as the newest emerging paradigm to thrive in the new complex world of work.

It is tempting to say that red, amber and orange are ego intelligent cultures and green and teal are eco intelligent cultures.

Although there are parallels; we position ego, eco and intuitive intelligence as the capacities required to preserve or evolve culture though the various types of consciousness and paradigms.

Each of these cultural paradigms emerges when the previous culture has reached a stage of 'stuckness' and something prompts the organisation (as explained by Laloux) to become aware of new ways of being and doing – this is where intuitive intelligence plays its part. In other words, an expansion of awareness or consciousness evolves, forming a new cultural paradigm. However, the previous stage elements do not disappear from the culture but rather become integrated within the next stage. So 'evolutionary teal' contains integrated elements of red, amber, orange and green. This expansion of awareness or consciousness contains the same development principles as our personal development journeys as outlined in Chapter 6 which we explained using the metaphor of the 'babushka Russian doll' (concentric circles figure in Chapter 6). Another similarity is the resolving of paradox at each stage that enables movement from one stage to the next. See the deeper dive at the end of this chapter for more on this.

If we start labelling leaders and cultures as good or bad, we are falling into the very trap we want to avoid. Each cultural paradigm has its value and contribution to make to the cultural blend of an organisation. Each of these cultures has a particular value or gift that it brought in order to escape the 'stuckness' of the previous paradigm.

The problem is not with the cultural paradigm itself but rather that organisations become stuck in a particular paradigm, losing the ability to evolve.

We stress that the point of cultural evolution is not to find the new cultural blueprint but rather to focus on the *process* of cultural evolution – the journey. This requires agility and an application of the three intelligences. The journey never ends, even as it travels through various destinations: each 'town' on this journey has a road leading in, and a road leading out. And each town lies within a bigger region, the prevailing context.

Agile cultures are responsive to the prevailing context

We mentioned in Chapter 2 (Rethinking leadership – the theoretical underpinnings) that many organisations are shifting their view of themselves from a well-oiled machine (amber and orange) towards that of a complex, living ecosystem (green and teal). The living ecosystem organisational metaphor implies that we can never really get to a point where culture becomes set or 'baked in' as there are so many forces at play all impacting on each other, and the context is shape-shifting continually.

It is necessary to start any process of evolving culture by 'getting real' about the current external and internal context. Leaders have to tune into and engage with 'what is' rather than pretend that things are better, or worse, than they are. This means to always have the organisational intuitive antennae on; sensing into the world, actively seeking new knowledge and trends in the world and in the industry. It also means applying eco intelligence to leverage the interdependencies between the internal and external environments. Our advice to leaders is always, "Start where your organisation and industry is at, "identify the stakeholders and harvest their inputs, their needs and the value they can add, then nudge them toward the next stage of development". If an organisation is clearly rooted in the amber paradigm, the worst thing would be to try and create a teal culture.

The emergence of a new culture has to be seen as a journey of *in-volvement* as well as *e-volvement* through the introduction of small changes that eventually form a larger groundswell and then become the new normal.

The challenge for leaders lies in adopting an attitude that is curious and interested, rather than negative and complaining. This often means shifting the organisational narrative from, for example, "The market is in chaos and there is nothing we can do about it" towards, for example, "How might we respond here – reinvent ourselves or think out-of-the-box?"

An important key to the successful evolution of culture is the ability to identify and respond to underlying polarities, many of which are paradoxical.

Agile cultures respond to fundamental organisational polarities

In Chapter 5 we referred to the ability of eco intelligent leaders to recognise and deal with polarities (some of which are paradoxical and messy), in a constructive way. The formation of the culture and structures is often an attempt to deal with the questions arising from the tension of underlying polarities. For example, quality vs quantity, external (customer) focus vs internal (products, staff) focus, control (centralisation) vs empowerment (decentralisation), short-term focus vs long-term focus, etc.

One common polarity we observe in many organisations is the ongoing organisational design question, "To what extent should we centralise (to satisfy the need for centralised control and fitting in) or decentralise (to satisfy the need for freedom and empowerment)?"

Many organisations follow a (usually 5 year) pattern – moving from greater centralisation to greater decentralisation. This swinging back and forth has a big impact on an organisation's culture because each of these paradigms carries its own underlying issues with trust and drives different attitudes and behaviours.

Another fundamental human polarity linked to this is the need for belonging (to feel part of the organisational family) vs the need for freedom and autonomy (to be left alone and given freedom to act).

We worked with a large business which had reaped the benefits of decentralising authority to various business units responsible for manufacturing of different products in the value chain. Each unit became very entrepreneurial, and profitable. However, over time, the need to harmonise things like performance management systems, procurement procedures and supply management triggered a quest for centralisation once again. The business units oscillated between their need for independence and the HO need for economies of scale through centralisation of certain functions.

Although a number of the top leaders realised the need for interdependence between the two polarities, they just could not figure out how to do both. They lost much of the entrepreneurial spirit in the business units when a large restructuring programme was launched. The installation of an ERP (enterprise resource planning) system by a large consulting firm did not make things any easier. The system became the new force that took the responsibility for the restructuring away from the leaders. In the end it was the consulting firm who reaped the benefits, with no clear upsides for the organisation.

A key test for cultural and leadership agility is the way the leaders deal with these paradoxes: their ability to think and create 'both-and'. In Chapter 5 we used the illustration of a circle and triangle and show how people often try to accommodate each other. The circle people try to fit the triangle ideas into their circle and vice versa. We describe this as 'pseudo agility'. One figure may grow bigger to fully accommodate the other but fundamentally they stay the same. Typical symptoms of pseudo agility are tolerance and accommodation of different cultures but no real integration (eco intelligence) of difference to create something new, the cone!

Figure 7.1

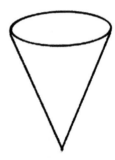

Figure 7.2

The story below demonstrates this point:

A medium-sized information systems consulting and training organisation (let's call them CS) operated pretty much like an ecosystem that self-organised through collegial, trust-based relationships and networks (green/teal). Engineers were continually being challenged to discover and develop their unique contribution and talents, within the context of the team and client needs. There was an unspoken expectation that all should share their ideas and intellectual property in order to increase the knowledge of the team as a whole. In this culture, it was frowned upon to hang onto things and to compete with or attempt to look better than colleagues. The unique strengths of each colleague were appreciated, and the team had to find ways to complement each others' strengths and weaknesses.

Sharing of knowledge and experience were strongly encouraged. The software industry had become very volatile and uncertain and CS was struggling to survive financially.

A large software house (let's call them GS) with an international footprint was attracted to the creativity and different approach of CS and bought the majority of shares in 2015. This gave them control of the company. They had a need to bring some 'freshness and innovative products' into the marketplace, hence their interest in CS.

Culturally, GS worked in a more traditional way. They have HR and financial systems and processes in place to monitor both individual and organisational performance, with little focus on self-managed teams and collaboration. Their organisation places high emphasis on profitability and scalability, to support their global footprint. CS staff and leaders were excited initially, because they saw an increase in financial security and opportunities to work globally.

The excitement did not last for long.

The CS staff were told that this was a 'merger' and a 'partnership' and that there would be no job losses. Yet, a major cost optimisation exercise resulted in 50% of the team being made redundant, plunging the remaining staff into fear for their jobs. Team work and self-organisation were replaced by clear hierarchical reporting lines and the CS Engineers were required to spend much time filling in management reports, tracking their activities per hour on a 'scorecard' that was to be used to determine their individual bonus at the end of the year. It was clear that this was not a partnership and trust and good will was quickly eroded. Some of the best engineers decided to leave because they could not relate to or support the new culture.

The organisation took a good two years to recover (not completely) and for the pendulum to swing to some middle ground where some elements of both started to be integrated, and a new culture started to form. The new culture is characterised by a strong 'orange – profit and product driven, competitive culture', with the remaining CS staff doing their best to restore the trust and to introduce some of the cultural elements they loved and cherished from the green/teal culture they knew before.

This is a good example of how agility and co-creation can disappear when tough business decisions are needed. Unilateral decision-making is introduced despite the plea for co-creation and transparency. The message is often, 'fit in or fly off' – the circle needs to fit into the triangle!

Genuine cultural agility is achieved when this kind of paradox is recognised as interdependent and is carefully managed.

Eco intelligence integrates the ego aspects of culture (e.g., a sense of belonging, security in a structured entity) and the intuitive aspects of culture (free thinking, autonomy, innovation and challenge) in the process of culture formation and transformation. It is the ability to have a both-and mindset where an organisation is able to reap the benefits of both whilst avoiding the traps of getting stuck in or overdoing either one.

A useful illustration of this is found in Barry Johnson's (1996)[2] concept of polarity management. Let us take the example of 'how decisions are made' which is often indicative of the type of culture. For example, are decisions based on *relationships* or on *rules/policies/processes*? The upside of rules is that they bring order, predictability and stability in an organisation but if the rules are overdone the organisation gets stuck and becomes rigid. When this happens, leaders are often sent on courses to develop their 'people skills' and 'emotional intelligence' to cultivate good relationships. When the relationship focus is overdone the organisation senses a need to develop more operating procedures and job profiles: more rules are put in place. The 'rules people' do not like the 'relationship people' because they fear chaos, and the 'relationship people' do not like the 'rules people' because they fear the claustrophobia that too many rules bring.

The inability to deal with this polarity leads to unnecessary conflict in organisations. Many organisations are trapped in this (infinity) loop that keeps them swaying from one side to the other as shown in the figure below.

However, if managed well, polarity and paradox can become a force for transformation in an organisation. Eco intelligence brings the ability to explore these paradoxes and to evolve cultures that hold elements of both.

An example of working constructively with polarity can be found in the pharmaceutical giant Roche. As a global company with more than 97,000 employees, it is on a journey to become a more agile organisation. In an interview with Gallup Managing Director Larry Emond, Chief People Officer, Cris Wilbur, and Global Head of Talent Innovation, Tammy Lowry, explains that for Roche agility means speed, flexibility and stability.

The process started with a leadership development initiative with their top leadership, which was focused on shifting mindsets, and to hold and leverage the polarity between flexibility and stability. Tammy Lowry explains the role of what we call eco intelligence in building speed and flexibility, "...the only way to effectively lead is to empower the people around you. That means your leadership role shifts from being director or approver to being a support function." Cris suggests that one of the anchors of stability (a counterbalance) is to be found in their culture and the values of integrity, courage and passion[3].

So, creating an agile culture starts with developing the 'agile mindset' of their leaders which enabled them to think into the third dimension and create a cone.

Culture and leadership – fit or misfit?

While culture is the result of the total collective expression of values, beliefs and practices, leadership is mostly vested in individuals who hold formal positions or who act as informal influencers. Like the two sides of the coin, leadership and culture have different 'prints' in that they are not just a reflection of each other. In other words, the value of the coin is the result of *both* sides being part of the coin.

Leadership always takes place within a cultural context and is either aligned (fit) or misaligned (misfit) with the culture. There is a creative, interdependent tension between leadership and culture – the one feeds on the other.

If this creative tension gets trapped in either side, both culture and leadership lose their impact. In other words, culture creates the context for leadership to function and leadership continuously helps to change and shape culture.

In our research we explored how leaders perceived this fit or misfit between their own leadership style and approach versus their organisation's cultural style and approach. We found some fascinating ways in which leaders went about addressing their perceived sense of not fitting. In order to identify this fit or misfit we asked leaders to score their current organisational and team culture by distributing ten points across Laloux's five organisational cultures outlined previously in this chapter (red, amber, orange, green, teal), and then to do the same exercise using the five colours to depict their personal leadership style and values.

We found four trends in how leaders responded to their sense of misfit with their organisational culture: *withdrawal, pseudo styles, activism and reflexivity.*

Withdrawal – and alienation

Leaders generally scored themselves higher than they scored their organisations on the 'green' values like care, empowerment and inclusion. In many instances this tension between the individual leaders and the organisation was bearable and even healthy. However, we found numerous cases where this misalignment had a significant impact on leaders' engagement and motivation. For example, there were leaders with a strong green and teal leadership orientation within a predominantly red and orange orientated culture, they reported a strong sense of alienation from their organisation.

> "I can't take this anymore."
> "I do not see a future for myself in this organisation."
> "I do my best, but do not get any recognition for the real value I bring."

Numerous leaders observed that the misalignment of individual leaders with the company culture was the main reason for good people leaving their organisation.

One such leader reflected:

> I'm realising that for me it is actually about legacy and about making a contribution. I'm still trying to decide what/where that would be, but I am certainly not finding it in this organisation!

We also found strong ego intelligent leaders struggling within a culture which emphasised care, collaboration, autonomy and interdependence (green/teal). They reported a sense of being 'out of control.' One leader mentioned what she called top management's 'delusion' in trying to introduce a new eco culture. She perceived a disconnect between the senior management team and staff: a lack of direction and control at the lower levels of the organisation. In our interview it became clear that she was seeing the world through the lens of her ego leadership style by assigning clear labels like senior and junior, of right and wrong, and a belief that leaders need to 'take a stand.'

We sometimes found that people lower down in the organisation structure had become addicted to management control and found it very difficult to take initiative. They expressed concerns such as, 'What will the boss say?' or 'Will I get fired if I do this or that without permission?'

Pseudo ego or eco intelligence – adopting the 'right' style

Let's take the phenomenon of psuedo agility one step further. Often the culture had an impact on what constituted the "right style" or "good leadership". For example, bringing strong direction, focus and drive was often criticised as "egocentric and domineering" in eco orientated cultures, while attempts at stakeholder engagement (eco intelligence) were perceived as "lacking in strong leadership" or "too slow" in ego orientated cultures.

We noticed that the misalignment between leadership styles and organisational culture had a significant impact on the leader's engagement levels and morale, as well as on the organisation's capacity to attract and retain leadership talent. This often led to anxiety, anger and other negative emotions. Further research is planned on this topic.

We uncovered an interesting phenomenon which we called *pseudo*-eco or *pseudo-ego* leadership where individuals spend time pretending to adopt a particular style (eco or ego) in order to fit in with the approved leadership approach.

This can be described as 'faking it': people play the cultural game to get approval from others, do what is expected, but they do not really believe it.

This was beautifully described by one leader:

> I find myself talking more, talking louder, listening less, desperately trying to get my voice heard because that's what is expected. If you don't get your point of view in there, you get side-lined as lacking leadership. I have noticed that I am losing myself in this process... I don't know who I am anymore!

Another leader described how the leadership team would sit for hours in their monthly meeting with their leader, all nodding away in apparent agreement and support but then fervently complaining about the meeting afterwards, "Well that was a load of nonsense, I would never in a million years think of doing the project that way!"

However, dwelling on the problem of misalignment is not going to help leaders dig themselves out of their hole of despair. We were interested in finding stories of leaders who actually did something about it! We found a few...

Activism – creating a sub-culture

Some leaders are wonderfully skilled at creating a department sub-culture (within the bigger organisational culture) within which they could give fuller expression of their style and values. For example, one leader in the utilities industry in the UK explained how he won accolades from top management for performance improvement through cost savings, using predominantly eco leadership in his division within a largely bureaucratic, top down (ego) culture:

> I did this with virtually no change of resources: it involved changing my people's mindset. I didn't introduce new technology or processes but simply evolved the culture in my division to one of more autonomy and care. I invited people to step up, to bring ideas and solutions, not problems, and then publicly and privately showing appreciation. It is so simple...just being more human, I suppose.

His bottomline results were far better than those of his colleagues. His results greatly increased his credibility and his department became known as 'the team to work for'. Sadly, when he tried to replicate his approach to initiate transformation across the greater organisation, the senior leadership could not understand what he was trying to say or do, as they were too strongly rooted in their need for centralised control. They were more interested in his team's results than the approach which achieved the results. He felt he was bumping against an invisible barrier and eventually, out of frustration, left the organisation.

Many years ago, Colin attended a conference on the theme of Total Quality Management (TQM). One of the keynote speakers was a Rear Admiral from the US Navy with responsibility for logistics and fleet supply in the Pacific Ocean. He described how he had used the principles of TQM to improve performance in his area of responsibility. A member of the audience asked, "How did you get permission to implement this kind of empowering approach in an organisation that relies heavily on command and control structures?" His reply, which with hindsight is obvious, was "I didn't ask for permission!"

This is perhaps a salutary lesson in how to go about creating a culture which is more empowering, where responsibility is delegated, where people at lower levels take more responsibility, where coaching and initiative are encouraged. You behave in the way you want others to behave.

This of course is easy to say and much harder to do. A leader may feel isolated, lonely, exposed and under threat if they are looking to develop a culture which is at odds with the prevailing organisational culture or the approach wanted by their boss. They may feel like a square peg in a round hole.

Reflexivity – 'dancing with culture'

At an individual level, the leader has some options if they feel like a square peg in a round hole. One is to leave that organisation (and the boss!) and look to join an organisation in which the culture is more aligned to their values, where their efforts will be recognised and valued. A second might be to change their approach to fit in. Fitting in would represent 'reflective' leadership in that the leader makes sure that their behaviour is always a reflection of the culture. This may or may not feel comfortable depending on how closely the leader's values and style resonate with the organisational culture.

Over time, leaders who perceive a 'misfit' with the culture and who constantly attempt to change their behaviour to fit the culture become exhausted and experience a sense of alienation from the organisation.

Reflexive leadership emerges when leaders believe that they have margin for manoeuvre, and they find a way to *dance* with the organisational culture. Leaders in this space fully realise the interdependent nature of leadership and culture. This means an ability to reflect on the interdependent relationship between the culture and themselves, noticing how the culture continually impacts and changes them and how they are continuously impacting and changing the culture. They realise that leadership and culture are truly two sides of the same coin. The biggest impact of reflexive leadership is the realisation that there really is no "them and me", but that "I am them, and they are me", and my attitude and behaviour has a direct impact on either preserving (pull back) or evolving (pull forward) culture every day, whilst at the same time being shaped by the culture. And this is where the application of ego, eco and intuitive intelligence in an integrated way can be very useful.

We met a leader with a teal mindset trapped in a red and amber culture, who had clearly learned to dance with the culture. He demonstrated significant results in cost saving through the application of self-organisation and empowerment (teal) instead of applying command and control (red/amber). These results got the attention of top management and gave him much credibility and a platform to share his 'recipe' for success and this influenced others to work in different ways.

He learned to play the game before he tried to change the game.

Let's now explore how leaders can use ego, eco and intuitive intelligence to preserve or evolve organisational cultures.

The impact of ego intelligence: culture as a blueprint

Within the ego paradigm, culture is viewed as a blueprint for behaviour. This blueprint is a result of 'institutionalised behaviour', when beliefs, norms and values become embedded in an organisation, community or society as 'the way we do things'. This is why it was very fashionable in the twentieth century (and even today) for a top team to formalise a clear vision and set of values as part of a strategy development process.

The vision and values are then communicated to all levels to obtain 'buy-in'.

The values are sometimes integrated into a performance management system using 360 feedback to measure alignment. This mechanism is used to gain the needed control or influence over which behaviours are sanctioned and which are not.

Some of the positive characterises of an ego 'intelligent' culture are a sense of a common identity, pursuance of a shared vision, loyalty to the organisation's brand, embellishment in the language and symbols used, and inspiring leaders – who are embodied examples of the culture. In this type of culture, the role of leader is to give recognition and approval to people's behaviour so that the culture becomes a safe haven. The need for compliance and to 'fit in' are strong drivers that reinforce the culture.

When it comes to recruitment of people or mergers and acquisitions, ego intelligent cultures will look for a cultural fit.

They may go to great lengths to ensure that new people or a new organisation fit in to the culture. However, this cultural safe haven may become a prison when people become stuck in their ways and addicted to their leaders. People may not want to take brave steps to solve problems in new innovative ways because they worry about what the boss will say and could even fear losing their jobs if they challenge things too much.

In an ego orientated culture, the voice of top management is critical when cultural change is required, and "agility" is more a matter of the leader's mindset than of the culture itself. In reality, an agile mindset cannot really be instilled from the top down. At most, agile processes can be driven from the top, but this always requires buy-in from the lower levels, which is not very often achieved because they lack a genuine sense of ownership.

The strength of an ego intelligent culture is its ability to shape and ground the attitudes and ways of doing, giving people a sense of common identity. The downside of an ego orientated culture lies in its 'stuckness' and inability to change, and its reluctance to release the energy and power of its people during a process of change.

The impact of eco intelligence: culture as a sensemaking process

An eco intelligent view of culture is different. It does not view culture as a blueprint for behaviour but as a *process* of sense (or meaning) making, that is socially constructed. In other words, it emerges from continuous human interaction. In Laloux's words, it involves the process of 'co-sensing and co-responding' with others. Culture is regarded as fluid in that it changes as people respond to each other and to the outside world. As the philosopher Heraclitus around 500 BC famously said, 'You cannot walk through the same river twice'[4].

These changes can sometimes be very subtle, yet transformational, as empowered leaders and teams co-sense and co-respond to disruptions. This is possible only if the organisation has created forums and processes that enable teams to make decisions and respond at speed in an empowered way, without having to wait months for their recommendations to be approved by the senior leaders. It implies a rewriting of the rule book – that new ways are discovered for cross-functional collaboration and for decision-making. For example, the *advice process* described by Laloux, where any person or team is enabled to make decisions once they have sought the advice of at least four experts on the subject, inside and outside of the organisation. It also implies that everyone is aligned with and following the same purpose, albeit that they get there in a different way.

A defining feature of an eco intelligent culture is the way in which inclusion of diversity is dealt with as discussed in Chapter 5. Eco intelligence enables the organisation and leaders to embrace the so-called misfits and to see them as opportunities to explore new ways of thinking and acting. In an eco intelligent culture people do not feel safe because they 'fit' but because they know that others embrace them because of their differences. They are not only tolerated but invited to share even radically different ideas.

In an eco intelligent culture, the *fear* of not fitting in has been replaced by *curiosity* about new ways of doing things.

Eco intelligence brings agility and diversity right into the centre of culture because it opens up spaces for new thinking.

The downside of an eco intelligent culture is that it can overdo challenge and innovative thinking at the expense of the structure and convergence required for implementation.

The impact of intuitive intelligence: culture as a part of something bigger

Intuitive intelligence sees an organisation as a part of something bigger. Organisational culture emerges as people sense into new ways of doing things, often on the spur of the moment, bringing 'big surprises' as Berger and Luckman (1966)[5] refer to it. These intuitive insights do not necessarily come as a result of a planned process of creativity or discussions but often as part of unplanned genius. If a culture invites these flashes of insight and recognises them when they come, more people will have their intuitive 'sensors' out. An idea will only stick if it resonates with others and a groundswell of support is formed. Those ideas that resonate with others will quickly gain support and go viral in the organisation's social media or old school grapevine.

One never knows beforehand how a new initiative will land with the organisation as there is no formula for an idea going viral. It is the result of touching an intuitive cord or resonance with others.

As said above, these new ideas or ways of doing things are sometimes small but in an intuitively intelligent culture they are encouraged.

Another quality of intuitively intelligent cultures is that they sense into the bigger purpose of the organisation: the 'why' of its existence – the difference it makes in the world. Intuitive intelligence brings an internal yearning for something bigger, something more or different to what we have now. This sense of purpose is more than a vision or a set of values, it provides a core source of energy that resonates with and aligns all the people and stakeholders of the organisation on a deeper level. For example, Whole Foods Market CEO Walter Robb:[6]

"We are not so much retailers with a mission as missionaries who retail. The stores are our canvas upon which we can paint our deeper purpose of bringing whole foods and greater health to the world." Every three years more than 800 store leaders gather to renew their purpose, to network, share experience and inspire each other.

Other characteristics include:

- Being truly open and asking for insights or perspectives that come intuitively from 'out there' – the wider industry, world trends
- Encouraging leaders to be more intuitive in the way they lead, trusting their gut feel, and listening to the intuition of their teams

Is there a best culture?

We are often asked, "which of these cultures is best?" or, "which of them achieve better results?" We have found, as with leadership, that an organisation too strongly rooted in one of these cultures to the expense of the others does not do well in the longer term. Ego heavy cultures lead to rigidity, silo mentality, and parent-child dynamics between managers and staff. Eco heavy cultures often end up with inertia, a lack of clear and efficient decision making and conflict avoidance. An overly intuitive culture that relies too heavily on tuning in to 'what's out there' may be insufficiently grounded and undervalue the importance of conserving the reliable traditional methods. As we argued above, the key to a 'good culture' is not in the blueprint, but how well the process evolves.

An agile culture is the result of all three intelligences playing together in the symphony of the cultural process. An intuitively intelligent culture gives people the wings to fly, ego intelligence builds the nest and eco intelligence makes sure that the wings are not clipped.

Speaking of wings, we will conclude by taking you back to the metaphor of the caterpillar becoming a butterfly. When the new cells carrying the DNA of the butterfly start to appear, the immune system of the caterpillar sees them as invasive and kills them. But these new cells continue to multiply and with time start to cluster together until the immune system of the caterpillar cannot eliminate them any longer. They start to disintegrate, allowing the new butterfly to form!

Depending on which of the leadership intelligences is strongest for you versus what your organisation values within its culture, you may feel discomfort. You may be one of the emerging cells, carrying the DNA of a new way of being, or you may be part of the immune system, holding back, clinging to recipes of past success. Fitting in or not could be seen as a curse or a blessing depending on the attitude you take towards it.

The story below is an example of how an organisation used all three intelligences at different times to transform their culture.

Bâloise, a European insurance group had enjoyed relative success for many years by following a standard operational excellence (Opex) strategy. Four years ago, the senior leadership team began to realise that to thrive in the complex new world of work, focusing on operational excellence was simply not enough. Operational efficiency needed to be matched by an equal focus on sustainable growth and the agility to adapt to an ever-changing business environment. To address this the CEO initiated a study tour to explore leading growth practices in different organisations in diverse countries and industries, including retail and banking.

An initial insight that emerged from this tour appeared too simplistic. A key finding was about the importance of leveraging the interdependencies between the staff, the organisation and the customers. Gert de Winter, CEO since 2016 said, "When I saw this, it seemed too simple. I felt quite silly even sharing it"[7]. However, this simple insight became the heartbeat of the transformational journey which was "Happy employees = happy customers = happy business (i.e., sustainable growth)".

The leadership team soon realised that while a lot of lip service was paid to customer relations, it was not really part of the company's DNA. There was a realisation that cultural agility and an agile mindset was a precondition for the transformational journey. A fictitious customer persona, 'Sarah', was created to enable leaders to step into the shoes of customers before making important decisions. Real clients were invited to share their experiences with groups of leaders. For example, a man who had lost a daughter was asked to share his story about how the insurance cover provided by Bâloise enabled the peace of mind he needed to grieve for his daughter.

It was also through this process of creating a more human narrative that the idea of 'Simply Safe' emerged as a core theme in the redesign of Bâloise. Simply Safe involved a repositioning from the traditional, transactional view of "we sell insurance policies" toward a more holistic approach and realisation of their business purpose, "We support customers in all aspects of their lives by providing safety"[8]. In order to offer safety, the company needed to be aware of the changing needs of customers and agile enough to stay relevant. This new theme involved a radical simplification of business processes, products, and communications and has led to repositioning and diversification of services.

Ego intelligent leadership: creating focus and inspiration

At the initial phase of the transformation journey the organisational culture was still quite top down and so the eco principles were driven by ego leadership to bring clarity of vision and direction. They adopted the benevolent ego intelligence to break through old habits and cultural paradigms that kept them back. Instead of using a command and control style, the leadership team decided to choose a more inspirational and fun style. Professional storytellers helped create the Bâloise story: a narrative describing the past and a potential future, written to capture the imagination of all staff and to communicate new core themes like employee and customer focus as well as Simply Safe.

The next step was for the leadership team to kick off a cascade of workshops throughout the organisation. A core feature of the resulting 'engage workshops' was for a team leader to tell the Bâloise Story in his or her own words and to then engage their team in a dialogue on how the team would implement it for themselves. This is where the shift towards eco leadership really started. Instead of getting 'buy-in' through selling their ideas, they created 'ownership' through collaboration and co-creation. Three interdependent elements were skilfully woven together by Bâloise to underpin the transformational process. Without a conducive organisational climate (soil), employees would not be prepared to risk making mistakes through experimentation (bets), and without the core business (source of income) remaining solid, the needed financial security for experimentation would not exist.

Eco intelligent leadership: viral change via 'sparks'

The senior team realised the importance of leveraging the influence of the informal leaders distributed across the organisation at all levels. They conducted an 'organisational network analysis' which involves a survey of all 7,000 employees asking two simple questions, "Who in Bâloise are you most likely to listen to?" and "Who are you most likely to be influenced by?" Three hundred informal influencers/leaders were thus identified and fondly named 'sparks.' These sparks were approached and invited to form a community to bringing about 'viral' change. Put simply this meant naturally getting others to "catch" the virus of new ways of behaving.

The sparks had a mandate to search for innovative ideas (drawing on intuitive intelligence). They were empowered to do whatever they felt was necessary to bring about the change of culture. Because they were not part of formal line management, and had this open mandate, managers took their ideas seriously and were agile enough to adopt them into the culture.

These sparks have since become an integral and important part of the journey. They simply live the new behaviours in all their interactions and are trusted by the senior leaders to do what they feel is needed.

The following are a few characteristics of the new agile culture:

Greater empowerment of teams and networks versus individuals

This is a move towards new ways of working such as agile and self-organised teams but also explicit changes in performance management with recognition based on team performance being as important as individual performance.

Greater informality

The company's bi-annual Top Leaders Conference has been renamed the Top Leaders Camp and now includes activities like making music together, storytelling, appreciative inquiry, peer coaching, fishbowls, and creative brainstorming around collaboration.

Innovation and experimentation

The 'bets' part of the business has initiated numerous ventures that run apart from, but in parallel with, the core business. In these ventures, staff are encouraged to experiment with new ideas and learn from their mistakes. Once a new idea has proved to be successful, it is then integrated into the core business.

In summary, the intuitive and simple formula of 'happy employees = happy customers = happy business' required some top-down benevolent ego leadership to provide the initial momentum and has been enhanced and embedded through eco leadership building the Bâloise Story: the co-created transformational journey.

The results so far

Bâloise has since enjoyed some impressive results on the group level, strong growth in all target segments, a solid balance sheet and a steadily increasing dividend for the shareholders.

This chapter in a nutshell

The cultural identity of any collective is made up of shared assumptions about how things work and how things should be done. These underlying (often unconscious) assumptions lead to shared values which in turn drive behaviours.

We referred to the work of Frederic Laloux and his explanation of various cultural paradigms and argued that when a culture becomes problematic it is because it gets stuck in a *blueprint* of past success. The three intelligences, applied in a synchronous way, will bring a *process* of cultural agility and enable organisational growth and transformation.

The keys to creating agile cultures lies in:

- Not getting stuck in seeing culture as a blueprint for behaviour, but rather as a continuous process that is co-created
- Being able to read and respond to external (the world, industry) and internal (current culture) context
- Being responsive to the fundamental paradoxes inherent in the organisational climate, for example the need for belonging (fitting in) and the need for freedom and empowerment

Most leaders perceive a fit or misfit with their organisation's culture. They respond by either withdrawing and sometimes leaving, pretending to fit in 'pseudo leadership', or becoming activists by attempting to change the culture by creating sub-cultures.

Some leaders develop the capacity to be reflexive. They realise that culture and leadership are two sides of a coin in that there is a creative, interdependent tension between leadership and culture and if this creative tension gets trapped in either sides, both culture and leadership lose its impact.

There is no best culture, culture is a continuous evolution indicative of the mindset, values and behaviour of its people. Reflexive leaders who realise this interdependence between themselves and the culture are able to draw more consciously on ego, eco and intuitive intelligence to provide what is needed in them as leaders, in response to their culture.

Reflection and application

- How would you describe your organisational culture in terms of Laloux's levels and ego, eco or intuitive cultures?

- To what extent do you perceive a fit or misfit between your leadership approach and the organisation culture?

- Do you feel that you are able (with others) to respond to and influence the prevailing culture?

- How might you do this using ego, eco and intuitive intelligence?
  - What might be a small first step?
  - Who do you need to get support from, and how will you get this support?
  - How will you know that you and others have made an impact?

A deeper dive

The work of Frederic Laloux in his book Reinventing Organisations is based on the work of Clare Graves. This deep dive is for those who are interested in and acquainted with the work of Graves and Don Beck, and some of the underpinning philosophies like Hegelian dialectics, Spiral Dynamics, Complexity thinking and Holism.

This will be more fully explored in a white paper following the publication of this book.

Laloux's levels and Graves's Spiral Dynamics (Beck, D, Cowan, C (1996)[9] use different colours to depict the levels of consciousness. For example, both use red for the power, Laloux uses amber and Graves blue for the next stage, both use orange and green, but for the stage after green, Laloux uses teal and Graves yellow. The stage after yellow is turquoise which is not part of the Laloux model.

For this discussion we draw on the work of Claudius Van Wyk who eloquently brings together the various thought traditions explained above in (inter alia) Chapter 6 of the book 'Moving forward with Complexity' (Tait, A.(ed.) & Richardson, K.A. (ed.) (2011).[10] Relevant to our work, is how he points out that the evolution from one cultural level to another is both a matter of form (the identifiable colours or stations on the journey) as well as process (the fuel in the tank) which spells out how the journey unfolds.

Regarding the process, we have argued its importance as the driving force in both Chapters 6 (personal development) and 7 (cultural development) in how we or organisations need to resolve the underlying human paradoxes, like our need for belonging versus our need for freedom and self-expression, our need to hold onto and our need to let go.

Van Wyk points to another important paradox as articulated by Graves: the needs of self (expressive – expansion – we express our needs) of red, orange, yellow and the needs of the collective (sacrificial – we sacrifice ourselves to the collective) of the alternative beige, blue, green. He refers to these also as expansion and containment, which resonates with the cosmic electromagnetic forces that underlie the evolution of the universe.

Our eco intelligence gives us the capacity to spot the underlying paradoxes and how they play out in our specific context, in our families, our business and the societies in which we live. These underlying tensions, for instance, are playing out in the cultural challenges in the USA and in the Brexit dilemma in the UK today. The way that leaders deal with these dilemmas will lead to regression to the lower levels (Graves's orange and blue) but will progress to higher levels of Graves's green and yellow, as integration takes place at a higher level.

Regarding the form, van Wyk points out that the ego consciousness can get fixated in the red and the orange levels and even yellow consciousness (in Graves's terms, the expressive or expansion energies) and that the eco consciousness is more rooted in the sacrificial and containment energies, that manifest on the blue, green and later turquoise levels of consciousness.

Intuitive intelligence is not something that wakes up later in life as part of the evolution of human consciousness. It is present from our birth, always tuning into and sensing its connection to the oneness or bigger whole, beyond the current realities of our culture or even our business. So, intuition functions at all levels of consciousness and values expression, sometimes expressing itself in futurists' experiences of probabilistic potentialities based on the unconscious detection of emergent patterns, and sometimes looking far into the future.

Notes

1 Laloux, F. (2014) Reinventing Organisations: A Guide to Creating Organisations Inspired by the Next Stage of Human Consciousness, *Nelson Parker*, Brussels.
2 Johnson, B. (1996) Polarity Management, *HRD Press*, Amherst, MA.
3 https://www.gallup.com/workplace/248714/roche-helps-leaders-achieve-power-agile-mindset.aspx
4 https://www.brainyquote.com/quotes/heraclitus_107157
5 Berger, P. L. and Luckmann, T. (1966) The Social Construction of Reality, *Anchor Books* and *Doubleday*, Garden City, NY.
6 Hutchins, G. and Storm, L. (2019) Regenerative Leadership, *Wordzworth*.
7 Olivier, S., Fleming, K., Hölscher, F., and Holton, V. (2019). Ego, Eco and Intuitive Leadership...A New Logic for Disruptive Times, *Hult International Business School*.
8 Olivier, S., Fleming, K., Hölscher, F., and Holton, V. (2019) Ego, Eco and Intuitive Leadership...A New Logic for Disruptive Times, *Hult International Business School*.
9 Beck, D. and Cowan, C. (1996) Spiral Dynamics, Mastering Values, Leadership, and Change, *Blackwell Publishers Ltd.*, Oxford.
10 Tait, A. and Richardson, K. A. (eds.). (2011) Moving Forward with Complexity: Proceedings of the 1st International Workshop on Complex Systems Thinking and Real-World Applications, *Emergent Publications*, Litchfield Park, AZ.

Chapter 8

Being an agile leader – what is your blend?

Effective leaders are able to sense into a situation and use the most appropriate leadership approach in the moment

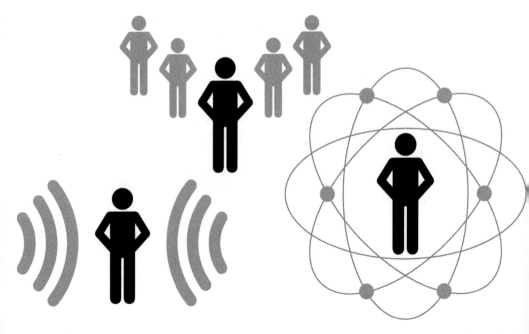

The art of leadership is in the blend

In this chapter we explain how agile leadership depends on developing a good blend of ego, eco and intuitive intelligence. We demonstrate how the three work together within the *process* of leadership and illustrate how different organisational contexts require a greater or lesser focus on certain leadership intelligences. At the end of the chapter we offer access to an *on-line self-scoring diagnostic* for you to assess your own (current) unique blend of ego, eco and intuitive intelligence.

Let's start with re-capping the distinguishing features of the three intelligences, summarised in the table below:

Element	Ego Intelligence	Eco Intelligence	Intuitive Intelligence
Describing word	Shaper	Integrator	Sensor
How this intelligence makes sense of the world	By defining and relying on clear analysis, categories, boundaries, and definitions	By co-sensing and co-creating meaning with others (socially constructed meaning)	By drawing on non-rational 'knowing', e.g., 'gut feel', heart knowing, and the quantum field
Identity	Self-me (including my team, my organisation, my country) as unique and separate from others. Separation	Self-we, as an integrated and interdependent part of the bigger ecosystem Integration	No-self. Oneness and separation as an illusion Wholeness
Over-arching capability	To shape the organisation according to our need, to define it, create boundaries and make sense of it	To understand the ecosystemic nature of the organisation and integrate diverse things and people to co-create and innovate	To bring new perspectives and insights-tapping into a space of unlimited possibilities

Element	Ego Intelligence	Eco Intelligence	Intuitive Intelligence
Cognitive skills (head)	Convergent and linear thinking	Divergent, convergent and emergent thinking. Matrix thinking. Integrative thinking and polarity management	Thrives in divergent thinking space, non-rational ways of knowing, wholeness, seeing patterns (connecting dots in new ways), sensing, foresight
Emotional skills (heart)	Creating emotional security and belonging by instilling pride through identity with group	Building trust through understanding, creating psychological safety, moving from fear to curiosity-promoting diversity, feeling part of, *because* I am different	Sense of connectedness, Excitement about what 'could be' Conviction
Action skills (hands)	Making things happen, creating structures and boundaries. Ensuring focus and speed	Allowing things to happen, group facilitation, enquiry instead of advocacy, empowering others to act	Intuitive decision-making, being provocative, experimenting and innovating

The three intelligences are interdependent

The three intelligences together can be seen like strands of DNA.

They are wound around each other, combining to work most effectively. This creates truly agile leadership, drawing on the best of the intelligences in a way that optimises their potential in any given situation. The successful integration of the three intelligences offers leaders the greatest potential to transform themselves and their organisations.

A common question we get asked by leaders is:

Can leaders be strong in all three intelligences?

Most people will feel more comfortable with one or perhaps two of the intelligences. This is often related to the way they see the world or the way they make sense of things.

Our leadership orientation develops over many years and is impacted by our upbringing, our values and our life experiences.

It becomes our internal logic for choosing a leadership approach: a way of behaving. For some people this feels natural because it has been deeply embedded as 'the right way to do things' and they may never call it into question. Indeed, when presented with alternative leadership approaches, they can be quite dismissive, seeing only their downsides and disadvantages.

It is normal that people have a preference, based on their assumptions about how things work and therefore what response is required. We all hold and need assumptions: they are like shortcuts to living and doing. If we had to go back to first principles and rethink every decision we make or every action we take, we would not survive! It is also normal to hold these assumptions quite firmly: they have served us well, maybe caused us to be successful over many years, so we are not going to throw them away easily. And yet there is a risk that we repeat patterns of behaviour based on assumptions that may or may no longer be valid.

In order to learn and grow people need to stop, reflect and challenge themselves about the relevance of their assumptions, mindset and ego stage development. They must be willing to hold their assumptions more lightly in order to experiment with other approaches or leadership intelligences, especially in the light of changing circumstances.

The process of experimenting with a different leadership intelligence involves making sense of a situation in a different way and can be quite uncomfortable initially.

Old certainties need to be released while the skills required to implement a different approach may not yet be developed – or at least not fully developed. As the famous American actor, cowboy, journalist and social commentator Will Rogers said, "It's not what we don't know that hurts. It's what we know, that ain't so!"[1]

The leadership model adopted in most organisations for many years is broadly based on ego intelligence. As we write, a number of leading organisations are trying to develop a more eco intelligent approach in order to become more agile: able to adapt and change quickly in today's unpredictable world. As well as being an organisational development effort, this requires individual leadership development to acquire the skills of the 'eco' leader and a change of approach in performance management, engagement and collaboration in order to encourage and reward different behaviours. In fact, it requires development at all levels as behavioural changes are needed across the organisation, not just within the leadership population.

A global financial services company we work with has consciously chosen to move towards a more eco leadership approach. One leader, responsible for about 250 people in multiple finance teams across several locations, talked of the difficult transition.

We have been on this journey for about two years. Some people love the new approach. They relish the increased responsibility and autonomy. They are quite confident when challenging business leaders in other divisions to explain their decisions or assumptions. Others claim to be happy but will always try to get me involved in the challenging conversations with senior people in the business. My problem is that because we removed layers of management, we no longer have the

> resources for people to refer decisions and problems upwards – they must take more initiative and responsibility at their own level. We are a traditional function in a traditional industry and this kind of change creates anxiety amongst long-serving staff. They are technically capable and I don't want to lose them but I am struggling to get them to really change.

Many of the leaders in our research expressed an underlying concern about their organisations, or the unwillingness of their boss, to experiment with different ways of thinking and working. There is perhaps a negative and positive cycle of opportunity at play here.

The negative cycle is that, in the face of uncertainty, leaders feel the need to respond by providing reassurance, a sense of security, continuity or even promises of more stable times ahead.

This cannot work. As it fails, 'the music gets louder' as leaders attempt to prove that it is working – which is what people want to believe! It cannot work because leaders are treating people like parents might treat children, not allowing them to take responsibility, not challenging them to step up to new opportunities and difficulties thereby reducing the possibility for movement, responsiveness and growth.

In the positive cycle, leaders see their role as helping people understand the reality of the paradox they face.

Despite a desire for predictability and reassurance, people need to step up into 'adult' mode and together find ways of working constructively with uncertainty. As they begin to do so more and more, a positive energy is generated which leads, through time, to greater capability to respond dynamically – and a more rewarding workplace for those involved.

The challenge is how to do this in an organisation which expects leaders to behave in a more traditional fashion, in other words, where leaders are supposed to know the answers, provide direction and keep things 'under control'.

We share two considerations to help leaders with this dilemma. It involves moving towards a more integrated use of the three intelligences. The first is to see leadership as a *process*, rather than an event or an action; and the second is that *leadership is always contextual.*

Leadership: a position or a process?

We invite you to see leadership as a process (as introduced in Chapter 2) and encourage you to notice where you might be lacking focus or energy.

How well are you enabling all three of these important processes: divergence, convergence and emergence to work in an interdependent way as you lead your team?

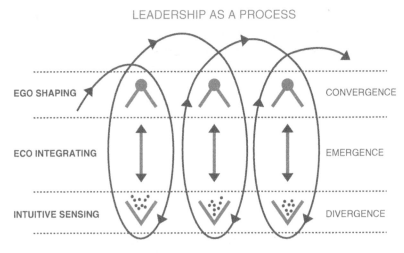

Figure 8.1 Spiral diagram depicting leadership as a process

The explanation below is taken from our observations of an IT team in the financial industry. It shows how an organisation or team can use agile project management processes to balance the three interdependent processes of divergence, convergence and emergence. It is also an example of 'distributed' leadership where the traditional role of the manager is replaced by three other, process focused, roles.

Agile project management

The Scrum framework is an agile project management methodology that works well in a complex, volatile and uncertain environment. The designers of the framework and programme Sutherland and Schwaber et al. (2001)[2] realised that the traditional approach to planning and executing large IT projects (top down 'waterfall' project management) did not work well for customers. Often when a new system 'went live', it was already out of date because the needs and requirements were signed off months or even years earlier and had changed in the meantime. This is the main reason why more than 70% of traditional waterfall projects fail to deliver the results that clients hoped for.

The Scrum framework replaces the traditional role of one project manager with three roles and applying the principles of iterative progress towards well-defined goals through teamwork and accountability. The *product owner:* who defines the project deliverables (or content) in conjunction with the customer. The product owners need high *ego intelligence* as their job is focused on delivering the agreed product on time (convergence). The *development team:* who use eco leadership principles like self-organisation, interdependence and agility in how the team works together, e.g., Scrum meetings are time-boxed, but highly participative, involves all key stakeholders for input, and are encouraged to think out of the box (divergence). The S*crum master:* who is responsible for the process, e.g., ensuring that agile values and principles are lived out and that there is sufficient communication between the stakeholders, checking that new ideas and suggestions have been properly recorded and understood by everyone. The 'Scrum master' must excel in *eco intelligence.* He or she needs to function like the corpus callosum in the brain which sometimes separates the right (creative brainstorming in Scrum meetings) and left brain (the sprint, getting things done) so that they can function *in*dependently, and sometimes integrates them to work *inter*dependently.

The process of agile project management is therefore a great example of the blended application of ego, eco and intuitive intelligence.

To summarise, ego intelligence (convergence) is initially used when clearly defining the roles and ring-fencing these roles. Each role self-organises and takes full ownership for delivery of its area of responsibility. Ego intelligence also brings focus to what is called a sprint (typically about 28 days) where no interference or opening up for new ideas is tolerated: something tangible needs to be delivered on time and within specification. However, when new, sometimes intuitive ideas emerge during a sprint they are captured in what is called a backlog and considered after the sprint. During the sprint there is considerable interaction and mutual support when required. For example, each day starts with a quick retrospection where the development team check-in with each other, asking three questions: What went well yesterday? What did not go well, and what can we do better? These meetings are held without interference or 'inspection' by the other roles.

After the sprint, and before the next sprint, the whole team have several 'Scrum' meetings to reflect on the product that has been delivered, and to learn. This retrospective process also includes defining the task for the next 'sprint'. Using eco intelligence this process integrates new ideas and takes evolving client needs into account considering the best way forward.

For Scrum to work well, a balance is required between ego capabilities (high focus on the task, delivery on time, and within budget) and eco capabilities (a mindset of interdependence and cooperation, sharing and listening in a transparent way). No blaming or shaming is allowed. People support each other because if one fails the whole team fails. Intuitive intelligence enables the team to stay connected with, and in tune with, the bigger whole (the organisation, the industry) which ensures that the work remains relevant and impactful, but also to allow for new flashes of insight to emerge and be considered for the next part of the project. A rigid project plan will not allow for this.

Leadership is always contextual

A popular expression says that, "If the only tool you have is a hammer, it's amazing how many problems look like nails!" An agile leader needs to know how to use the different intelligences appropriately and respond with what will work best, in any given situation or context.

We share a framework developed by Ralph Stacey (1996)[3] which outlines three different organisational contexts. This framework considers two contextual dimensions: the degree of *certainty* or lack of certainty about the business, the industry and the future, and the degree of *agreement* or lack of agreement between key stakeholders on what needs to be done and how to do it.

The first contextual space is called the 'simple space' where there is fairly low level of uncertainty and a high level of agreement about what needs to be done. The organisation can pretty much be run like a well-oiled machine. For example, a franchised coffee shop like Starbucks or Costa where little ambiguity exists about what

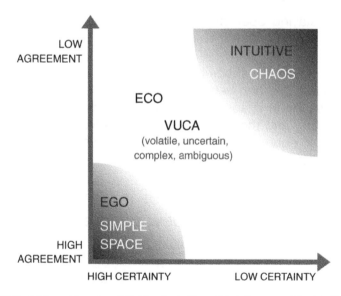

Figure 8.2 Certainty and Agreement Matrix adapted from Ralph Stacey and Patricia Shaw

to do and how to do it. Here more *ego intelligence* may be appropriate, leaders can set the vision and then manage through the cascading of KPIs with clear rewards and consequences for poor performance in place.

The second contextual space is one where the levels of uncertainty rose and the level of agreement dropped into what is often called the VUCA world (volatile, uncertain, complex and ambiguous). For example, the banking industry where there is much uncertainty about the future of banking as we know it today. There is significant digital disruption such as banking apps or blockchain and much disagreement about how to respond. Some leaders are clinging to the past while others are wanting to radically innovate. No one leader can claim to have all the answers. In this context more *eco intelligence* may be helpful.

Leaders in this context need to create spaces for generative dialogue where people can 'co-sense' and 'co-respond' with all their key stakeholders, including customers.

It means staying open and curious to what new thinking might emerge.

The third contextual space is one characterised by very high levels of uncertainty and very low levels of agreement. An industry or organisation in chaos. For example, the disruptions facing the hotel industry and the taxis with disruptors like Airbnb and Uber. And now of course, the COVID-19 pandemic creating chaos in many industries.

Here a good splattering of intuitive intelligence can enable a sensing beyond the current paradigms into the bigger world.

Following macro trends and weak indicators can bring fresh insights to reframe and re-invent the business model. Then eco intelligence is needed to integrate and consolidate perspectives, and ego intelligence to shape them into something new.

National culture contexts

One CEO told us how he realised he needed to use a different approach in a new business because of a culturally different context. After having run a successful business in a developed Western country for over 20 years, he acquired a business in a developing country in Africa. He discovered that many of the assumptions on which he had built the structured operating model for his first business did not work in the new acquisition. He simply did not understand enough about the cultural context to transfer his ego intelligent approach.

I found myself having to learn new laws, new rules and new legislation in a country that has experienced the brunt of 30 years of civil war. The people are struggling with poverty, a lack of education, fatherless homes, massive unemployment and very low skill levels.

Because he felt unsure and nervous about doing business in such a new context and with different people, he decided to get right into the day-to-day work operations, working closely with each of his direct reports' teams, in order to establish work processes and practices. He did this by listening to their ideas (eco), integrating diverse perspectives (eco), but then shaping them into concrete processes and practices, with supporting systems (ego) e.g., how to do a shift change, how to get the trucks logged, etc. This approach of generative dialogue is in contrast with the normal ego intelligent way of getting their 'buy-in' for his ways of running a business.

He did this for 18 months before feeling confident enough to take a step back and allow the leaders to continue in a more autonomous way. When asked about the impact of this intervention he said that a definite sense of trust and loyalty had been achieved during these 18 months because these leaders and teams appreciated that he was prepared to 'understand them' and to 'get his hands dirty'. He saw this period as one of co-crafting the way of work in this business which is clearly an application of eco intelligence but certainly with a good splatter of ego intelligence in shaping the co-created ideas into tangible structures and processes.

On reflection, he says that he adopted a completely different approach in this new business and has realised how detrimental it can be to "take a winning recipe from one cultural context and attempt to make it work in a totally new cultural context". He is now very aware of how the different leadership intelligences were called on from him in these two different environments.

He said that he is currently challenged to draw more on his intuitive intelligent to sense and understand some of the unspoken tensions are that are currently emerging in the leadership of this organisation, which he is finding challenging especially because he cannot be there physically due to COVID-19.

The impact of organisational culture

Determining the best blend of the three intelligences to use at any given time will also depend on contextual factors like how traditional or conservative the organisational culture is, the maturity of the team (or organisation), the time available, the leader's willingness to change or experiment, the need for innovation, risk or safety issues and many more.

On a recent project we helped an organisation to develop a more eco intelligent culture and leadership approach. The cultural context was a conservative and traditional family business where the elderly father was held up and respected as the 'father figure' (literally). The CEO, the son, expressed a desire to shift the culture into more of an eco culture. He wanted to empower his managers with higher levels of shared problem solving and decision-making as the business was expanding exponentially.

The father had a well-cultivated habit of micro-managing and interfering with managers and staff lower down the organisation. He regularly gave them instructions, interfered with their plans, or usurped the authority of line managers: often confusing workers as to whom to listen to. This unhelpful behaviour had often been brought to his attention, but he found it hard to change because his management style was so engrained. In his view, he could not trust managers lower down and said, "After all, it is my business in which I have years of experience!" We talked to him about 'servant leadership' and the value of asking versus telling. The words 'servant leader' resonated well with him in a general context as a keen Christian but he saw it as 'inappropriate within his family business'... "How can a leader possibly serve? Leaders need to lead and that means telling others what to do."

Realising that it would take tremendous time and effort to get him to change his ways, we decided to introduce clear reporting lines and guidelines to minimise his natural tendency of micromanaging. It was not ideal, but the context required clear, tangible rules and this was an approach he understood. We had to, for the first few months at least, work within the existing ego culture, using the familiar language of structures and reporting lines to bring about a change of behaviour. He was compelled to follow the rules and to assume a more strategic role while the managers lower down the organisation were empowered to lead their teams in the way they saw fit. In other words, we put top down structures in place (ego) to create a platform for an eco culture to develop but also started to empower the managers with knowledge and skills to run the business more tactically.

Leaders need to be finely attuned and responsive to both the external industry context and the prevailing organisational culture context. We indicated earlier which types of intelligence might be most helpful in the different contexts described by Ralph Stacey in his Uncertainty and Agreement framework. However, our research findings suggest that the application of the different intelligences is more subtle than just aligning them to a specific space on the matrix.

The relevance of ego, eco and intuitive leadership can be seen in terms of specific circumstances or certain conditions as follows:

Ego leadership appears most applicable when

- The objectives are clearly definable, the work processes and outcomes are simple, predictable and easily measured, and where less creativity or innovation is required.
- The team or organisation is facing a crisis and does not have the required information or emotional capacity to self-organise in order to deal with it.
- Teams or individuals lack the interest, capacity and/or maturity to self-manage.
- Teams are filled with insecurity and in need of a sense of direction.
- Speed or fast decision-making and action is needed.
- The organisation is stuck (not making headway) and requires a nudge to the next level or into a different direction (as illustrated in the example above).

Eco leadership appears most applicable when

- The environment is complex, volatile and uncertain and there are no obvious clear answers to problems.
- There is significant diversity of thought and even conflicting ideas.
- High levels of interdependent actions between teams or individuals are required for success.
- Potential for self-management is recognised and cultivated to a level where people have the maturity and capacity to self-organise.
- Information and knowledge is widely shared to enable informed decisions.
- A uniting and evolving common purpose is evident or possible.

- There is a need or will to develop an organisation that is less dependent on a single leader and more interested in the expression of leadership at all levels.
- Time can be allocated for generative dialogue, which is quite often a problem in the fast-moving business environment.

Intuitive leadership appears most applicable when

- There is a need to delight customers with creative thinking and new solutions.
- Use of historic data does not predict the future.
- More customer or stakeholder engagement may just produce 'more of the same' – as Henry Ford reportedly once said: "If I had asked my customers what they wanted; they would have asked for better horses."
- The organisation or industry is at the edge of chaos and the future landscape looks very different to the past.

Excellent in some and good enough in others – what is your blend?

Our research suggests that it is quite rare for one individual to be equally comfortable and competent with all three intelligences. Being too comfortable or getting stuck in one particular intelligence means that one runs the risk of looking at any situation through a frame that tells you that your preferred or natural intelligence is the one most suitable.

It is advisable to strive to be 'good enough' in *all* three intelligences in order to minimise the risk of this happening.

Being clear about your own preferences is a good starting point. We encourage you to use the *self-assessment diagnostic* at the end of this chapter (under reflection and application questions) to help confirm your personal blend or mix of preferences, then work through the reflection and application questions. These will help you to identify development opportunities to increase your personal leadership agility.

Recognising complementary strengths in others – the importance of distributed leadership

Within a team, it is quite possible for all three intelligences to be present. This represents a balanced leadership approach in which different perspectives are taken, ideas are evaluated against different criteria and seen through different lenses. It maximises the possibility of innovative solutions emerging while retaining a necessary degree of structure and involving other people in the leadership space as explained in the Scrum example above. It is commonly referred to as 'shared' or 'distributed' leadership. It applies as much to informal leaders stepping up and leading as it does to those in formal leadership roles.

We worked with an industrial equipment company in Germany that we feel had mastered the art of distributed leadership. They recognised and used diverse capabilities of each leader in the team in different situations. For instance, the one leader was an inspiring speaker, and was often invited by his colleagues to convey certain management and strategic decisions of the top team. Another leader was good in developing project plans. This team functioned well because they did not protect their own positions but worked together as an eco intelligent team.

Remember the Bâloise story of the informal 'sparks' in Chapter 7? Sharing the leadership space with one's team members regardless of whether or not they hold a formal leadership role, can have a massive impact on the morale and sense of empowerment experienced by at levels.

One of the challenges for leaders is to value the contribution of those who are different or even opposite to them. This is particularly true when the team is under pressure. Leaders with an ego intelligence preference may see more eco behaviours or ideas as 'interesting' or 'innovative' when all is going well but see them as a 'waste of time' or 'pointless' when the pressure is on to deliver to a deadline or stick within budget. Equally, eco intelligent leaders may value the clarity and efficiency of a more ego intelligent approach until it seems to be marching them in a direction which they believe to be wrong, leading to them withdrawing emotionally and sometimes even physically by resigning. This was reflected in a comment from a leader talking about her colleague, "He always says just what I don't want to hear, just when I don't want to hear it...and, frustratingly, he is usually shown to be right in the end!"

In closing this chapter, we return to the metaphor of the triple helix of DNA representing the three intelligences as interdependent strands which depend on each other in order to reach their potential. Just as the human body cannot flourish with only with a strong skeletal frame, so ego, eco and intuitive leadership are all ineffective on their own, but incredibly powerful when used together in the symphonic dance of leadership.

Even if you find it uncomfortable, we encourage you to recruit and work with leaders opposite or different to yourself. Also, to create diverse teams with members who complement each other to bring the important blend of ego, eco and intuitive intelligence to the organisation.

The stronger the blend of leadership, the more equipped your organisation will be to embrace the opportunities arising from the uncertainty of our world today.

This chapter in a nutshell

This chapter emphasised that agile leadership draws on developing a good blend of ego, eco and intuitive intelligence, and we provide a diagnostic tool for readers to assess their own unique leadership blend.

The three intelligences work together interdependently to enable the process of leadership which entails divergence (new thinking that moves beyond the boundaries of the situation), emergence (of new ideas) and convergence (taking new ideas into concrete action).

The use of the three intelligences is most effective and impactful when guided by and appropriate to the context of the national cultural context, industry context, the organisation culture and the maturity of the team.

Although it is not always possible for a single leader to be strong in all three, we encourage leaders to explore the idea of 'distributed' leadership by tapping into the diverse strengths of the whole leadership team as well as the informal leaders and networks, enabling the natural ecosystem to flourish, rather than controlling it.

Our leadership blend diagnostic: what is your blend?

To assess your leadership blend, please complete the self-assessment by typing this URL into your browser. It will take you to the Virtual Ashridge platform where the instructions are clearly explained. This is a self-assessment and takes about 20 minutes to complete. You will see the results immediately. Please do contact us if you would like to discuss or explore using this diagnostic in your organisation.

https://public.leadershiplive.hult.edu/section/leadership_blend

Reflection and application

We encourage you to spend time reflecting on your leadership blend, considering these questions:

- What was your initial reaction when you saw your result? (surprise, disappointment, confirmation of what you already know?)

- Which intelligence would you like to develop? Why?

- How might you develop this intelligence? (see the tips in each chapter on ego, eco and intuitive intelligence)

- Do you have a good blend of the intelligences in your leadership team? If not, what might you do to ensure a better blend? For example, how might you discover and enable the informal leadership networks more effectively?

A final word

As we thought about this book, we realised that we all carry the secret of agility in the palm of our own hands. We ask that you look at your hands – they are wonderful instruments that enable us to function, especially how our opposable thumb distinguishes us from all other mammals.

An ambitious young man once asked a successful business leader for the key to his success. The businessman held out his hand and said:

> It is all here in the palm of my hand. With my closed hand I can hold onto my money and my power; but it can also be a fist to fight or protect myself. Yet a closed hand cannot receive. Sometimes we must open our hand to give, because an open hand can also receive. An open hand can also reach out to others in an act of friendship, this is why one should shake as many hands as possible in business. You need the wisdom to know when to close and when to open your hand, and that I can't teach you.

We believe that the most effective leaders are those with this wisdom. Those who are able to effectively hold this polarity between ego (holding) and eco (releasing) intelligence; intuitively knowing when to close the hand, take control, move quickly and push things forward, and when to open the hand, and to release control, allowing your organisational ecosystems to flourish!

Notes

1 https://www.goodreads.com/quotes/296338-it-s-not-what-we-don-t-know-that-hurts-it-s-what
2 Schwaber, K., Sutherland, J., et al. (2001) A manifesto for agile software development, http://agilemanifesto.org/iso/en/manifesto.html
3 Stacey, R. (1996) Complexity and Creativity in Organisations. *Berret-Koehler*, San Francisco, CA.

APPENDIX:
ROBERT DILTS' LOGICAL LEVELS MODEL FOR EGO, ECO AND INTUITIVE LEADERSHIP

Levels	Ego intelligence		Eco intelligence		Intuitive intelligence	
	Gifts	Shadows	Gifts	Shadows	Gifts	Shadows
	When used appropriately	*When overplayed*	*When used appropriately*	*When overplayed*	*When used appropriately*	*When overplayed*
Behaviours "I do"	Leads from the front Creates focus by setting a clear vision and goals Provides security that things are 'in hand' Makes decisions quickly	Single mindedness – insist on my own way Creates distance through the use of status Critical of others' ideas Manages upwards 'to look good' Uses fear to get compliance	Creates space for collaboration and dialogue across boundaries Empowers teams to self-manage Includes and integrates diverse ideas and people	Procrastination Conflict avoidance Overly accommodating Inability to focus Inability to make things happen, inertia	Brings fresh insight and perspectives Challenges the status Explores new possibilities outside the normal paradigm	Ideas may lack 'grounding' in reality Single-minded, insists intuition is right Creates chaos by bringing too many unfounded ideas Loss of interest in an idea that counteracts their intuition

Levels	Ego intelligence		Eco intelligence		Intuitive intelligence	
	Gifts	Shadows	Gifts	Shadows	Gifts	Shadows
	When used appropriately	*When overplayed*	*When used appropriately*	*When overplayed*	*When used appropriately*	*When overplayed*
Competencies "I can"	Clear communication Influence through 'push' (directive) or 'pull' (inspiration) Clear and linear thinking Clear sense of right and wrong Create psychological safety through a sense of belonging (tribe)	Not defined as they show up under 'behaviours' above	Influencing through collaboration Process and group facilitation Coaching Engendering psychological safety Integrative thinking Polarity management	Not defined as they show up under 'behaviours' above	Influence through inspiration Big picture perspective 'Gut feel' Contemplative, mindful curious and experimental Imaginative	Not defined as they show up under 'behaviours' above Not grounded in reality Perceived as woolly or esoteric Impractical
Beliefs/Values "I believe"	People need a strong leader to show the way I must find the answers Providing certainty There is a 'right way' and my people should do the 'right thing'	People cannot be trusted Protect own reputation (at the expense of others) Leadership authority should not be challenged	Wisdom of the group, impossible for one person to have the best solution We are all connected and interdependent Separation is an illusion Leadership is successful when shared Growth mindset – curiosity	Lack of self-belief/confidence Too high expectations of others leading to unrealistic levels of empowerment Overly optimistic about the inherent good in all and the organisation system	'Oneness' everything is part of a bigger consciousness There are many ideas yet to be discovered There are non-rational ways of knowing Flashes of insight, dreams, synchronous events	

Levels	Ego intelligence		Eco intelligence		Intuitive intelligence	
	Gifts	Shadows	Gifts	Shadows	Gifts	Shadows
	When used appropriately	*When overplayed*	*When used appropriately*	*When overplayed*	*When used appropriately*	*When overplayed*
Identity/ Metaphor "I am"	A lighthouse showing my people the way to safety in a stormy sea A library, the source of knowledge and solutions A mother or father to my team, protecting them	Dictator King Alpha male/ female	Orchestra conductor, drawing on various talents to make music Gardener, ensuring fertile soil for the growth of all	Unsure of who I am Ocean in a storm, pulled in many directions by the tides	The all-seeing eye Antennae – tuning into signals 'out there' Sponge – absorbing and feeling	Prophet - able to predict things

INDEX

Note: **Bold** page numbers refer to tables and *italic* page numbers refer to figures.